THE LIVING
TRADITION

MOSES
HADAS

PERSPECTIVES
IN HUMANISM
Planned and Edited by
RUTH NANDA ANSHEN

Board of Editors

THE LIVING
TRADITION

MOSES
HADAS

Πάλαι δὲ τὰ καλὰ ἀνθρώποισι
ἐξεύρηται, ἐκ τῶν μανθάνειν δεῖ

 THE NEW AMERICAN LIBRARY

Library of Congress Catalog Card Number: 66-26041
Published by The New American Library, Inc.
1301 Avenue of the Americas, New York, New York 10019
Published simultaneously in Canada by
General Publishing Company, Ltd.
Printed in the United States of America

CONTENTS

PERSPECTIVES IN HUMANISM
THE FUTURE OF TRADITION—vii
RUTH NANDA ANSHEN

PERSPECTIVES IN HUMANISM
THE FUTURE OF TRADITION
RUTH NANDA ANSHEN

Perspectives in Humanism is designed to affirm that the world, the universe, and man are remarkably stable, elementally unchanging. Protons remain protons, and the other known elements are themselves, even when their atoms are broken; and man remains, in his essence, man. Every form of nature possesses what Aristotle called its own law. The blade of grass does not exist to feed the cow; the cow does not exist in order to give milk to man; and man does not exist to be subdivided, for to subdivide him is to execute him. Man is an organism, a whole, in which segregation of any sort is artificial and in which every phenomenon is a manifestation of the whole. The lawfulness of nature, including man's nature, is a miracle defying understanding.

Perspectives in Humanism submits that there is a constant process of continuity within the process of change. This process lies in the very nature of man. We ask ourselves: What is this constant? What is it that endures and is the foundation of our intellectual and moral civilization? What is it that we are able to call our humanistic tradition? What is it that must survive and be transmitted to the future if man is to remain human?

The answer is that this constant lies in recognizing what is changeless in the midst of change. It is that heritage of timeless and immutable values on which we can fix our gaze whenever the language of change and decline which history speaks seems to become too overwhelming for the human heart. It offers us the spectacle of the constancy of certain basic forms and ideas throughout a process of continuous social mutations, intellectual development, and scientific revolution. The constant is the original form maintaining itself by transformation and adapting itself to changing social conditions, the continuity which is the very medium of change.

It is the loss of awareness of this constant in our time, not through the failure but rather through the very success of our modern scientific and technological achievements that has produced a society in which it becomes increasingly difficult to live a life that is human.

Perspectives in Humanism tries to confront, and, if possible, show the way to the resolution of, the major dilemma of our epoch: the greatest affliction of the modern mind. This dilemma is created by the magnificent fruits of the industrial revolution on the one hand and by an inexorable technology on the other. It is the acceptance of power as a source of authority and as a substitute for truth and knowledge. It is the dilemma born out of a skepticism in values and a faith in the perfectibility of the mind. It accepts the results of scientific inquiry as carrying self-evident implications, an obvious error. And finally it defines knowledge as a product, accepting lines of force emptied of lines of will, rather than, as indeed it is, a process.

The authors in this Series attempt to show the failure of what has been called scientific humanism, to show the limitation of scientific method which determines only sequences of events without meaning and among these events none more meaningless than man. For modern science is not concerned with human experience, nor with human purposes, and its knowledge of ascertained natural facts can never represent the whole of human nature. Now man is crying out for the recognition of insights derived from other sources, from the awareness that the problem of mechanism and teleology is a legitimate problem, requiring a humanistic solution.

It has always been on the basis of the hypothesis that the world and man's place in it can be understood by reason that the world and man become intelligible. And in all the crises of the mind and heart it has been the belief in the possibility of a solution that has made a solution possible.

Studies of man are made in all institutions of research and higher learning. There is hardly a section of the total scholarly enterprise which does not contribute directly or indirectly to our knowledge of man's nature. Not only philosophy and theology, not only history and the other humanities, not only psychology, sociology, biology, and medicine investigate man's nature and existence, but also the natural sciences do so, at least indirectly, and even directly, whenever they reflect upon their own methods, limits, and purposes.

It is in the light of such considerations that *Perspectives in Humanism* endeavors to show the false antinomy between the scientist and the humanist and the Cartesian error of dualizing mind and body. This Series tries to point to the incoherence of our time which implies the breakdown of integrative relationships, and to demonstrate that in science, as in all other fields of human thought and action, humanism may be preserved only through channels of shared experience and through mutual hopes. Indeed, humanism in these volumes is defined as that force which may render science once more part of universal human discourse. In this, it is here proposed, lies the future of tradition. Our search is for the "ought" which does not derive from facts alone.

In many realms of scholarly work there is an awareness of the fragmentation of man. And there is an increasing recognition that the study of man-made and natural ecosystems is as necessary as the study of isolated particles and elementary reactions. Most impressive has been the reaction of many scientists to the problems of the "atomic age" created by the technical application of their own theories. They realize that the question of the human meaning of scientific research cannot be repressed any longer in view of the immensity of these problems.

In biology and medicine the qualitative uniqueness of every life process, and especially the uniqueness of that process which is called human, has come into the foreground of investigation. And, above all, biology, psychology, and medicine have made parallel efforts to overcome the accepted but untenable split between the psychological and the physiological aspects of human nature, remembering with Aristotle that the soul is the meaning of the body.

Historical studies in all directions, including political, social, economic, cultural, and religious history, have begun to ask the question: What are the characteristics of man as they are manifested in history? The exclusively factual and causal approach to history generally, and its special divisions such as history of the arts, of literature, of societal forms, of religion, has been broken down in many places. The question of meaning has not replaced the question of fact but has given research another dimension and a direct relevance for man's self-interpretation.

This is the situation. No convincing picture of man has arisen in spite of the many ways in which human thought has tried to reach it. But one thing has been achieved: The problem has made itself felt with great force in many places in spite of considerable resistance. This alone would justify a concentrated attempt to seek for preliminary answers and new questions resulting from them. And this is the aim of *Perspectives in Humanism.*

There is, however, another rather serious reason for cooperation in the study of this new and enlarged meaning of humanism. It is the fact that, under the impact of these developments, a linguistic confusion in all important matters of man's existence has taken place in the Western world—a confusion which makes cooperation extremely difficult. Most concepts used in scholarly attempts to draw a picture of man are ambiguous, or obsolete, or fashionable clichés. It is impossible *not* to use them, but they mislead if they are used. This is not a recent development —although the methods of contemporary publicity have supported it and are one of the greatest impediments to healing it—but it is a result of the intellectual and social history of the last centuries. A change is possible only if this history in all its ramifications is studied from the point of view of the disintegration of the language concerning man which has taken place in the last centuries. Such a dialogue is formidable and must be done in terms of a continuous exchange between representatives of the different spheres of knowledge and of cultures. It is our hope that this Series will provide favorable conditions for such an exchange.

The historical approach must be done in interdependence with a systematic approach. Concepts developed in one sphere must show their relevance for other spheres. This also is being done in a casual way in contemporary literature. It must be done methodologically. The departmental boundaries must be trespassed continuously. It is ultimately impossible to make a true statement about the physiological dynamics of the human body without taking into consideration the spirit which forms the flesh. It is ultimately impossible to describe the self-destructive tendencies in a neurotic person without describing the structures of estrangement in man's social existence. These examples can be increased indefinitely. They show that the departmentalization of our knowledge of man, although it was and is a matter of expediency, is at the same time a cause for distortion. Here lies the main positive task of *Perspectives in Humanism*.

Humanism is the ideal pattern supposed to reveal the true nature of man and the task for which he was born— the task of shaping himself into a true man and thereby creating a society worthy of him to be transmitted to future generations. For humanism is a lasting truth, not merely a transitory historical phenomenon. Like the changeless *logos* of which Heraclitus spoke, it pervades the whole process of eternal flux, and may even be said to be like a divine fire that works in each of us whether we know it or not. There stands behind our Western tradition, just as behind the great traditions of the East, a common metaphysical faith which transcends all schisms and conflicts within it.

And just as humanism means that there exists a common humanity beyond all divisiveness, so humanism also means that a unitary nature unites scientist and humanist alike. It can no longer be said that man is either a scientist or a humanist. The knower and the known, the doubter and the doubt, are one. To identify the scientist with a single method, the scientific one, that is, with a single procedure, is a distortion of science. All the powers of the mind, of intuition, of observation (to which the observer brings his own perception), of discursive and nondiscursive knowledge, are brought into play in the achievement of scientific interpretation. And the pre-analytic data of science, if called "facts," are in reality but problematic facts. The only facts initially given for exploration are the facts of humanistic relevance, facts laden or saturated with loose or crude interpretations and demanding therefore reinterpretations by procedures free from what Bacon described as idols of the mind.

The difference between humanistic and scientific meaning is a difference not of kind but of degree. Can it be seriously maintained that, prior to the advent of scientific knowledge, with its elaborate hypotheses and theories, all intent upon the search for the nature of things, men were acquainted merely with sense data, or meaningless impressions? Prescientific knowledge is also knowledge, involving in incipient or inchoate form most of the activities in which science is engaged, such as naming and classifying, numbering and measuring, describing and explaining. And all these aspects are but the humanistic yearning in man's nature to establish a legitimate place for himself in the cosmic scheme from which he feels that he has been estranged. However far-flung its hypotheses or comprehensive its theories, science has no objects for its application save such as can be known through a humanistic interpretation and therefore known through perception suffused with judgment and belief. Science plunges into the phenomena, isolated and apart from the wholeness of reality, interpreting with precision and even accuracy and by devices that make possible more adequate inferences, and sometimes even more reliable predictions, the very same world of things which are antecedently recognized through the implicit perceptions of humanistic insights.

What this Series hopes to demonstrate is that humanism by its nature is intent upon forcing the mind to make, since it is unable not to make, judgments of value. It is to accept once more the validity of the metaphysical hypothesis. What humanism desires and demands is an insight into the meaning of the universe of nature and of man as totality by the use of categories more general or pervasive than those required for the things segmented by a special science. The antihumanist prejudice, prevalent in certain quarters, can be explained only by the dogma that the universe and man in it are everlastingly divided among and by the special sciences, the synopsis of each being separate and exclusive so that a categorial synopsis of the total nature of the thing remains *a priori* precluded.

It is the endeavor of *Perspectives in Humanism* to show that there is no knowledge (knowledge which is synonymous with being) save by a humanistic perception of what we know. For we bring ourselves to every objective act of cognition, we are always intimately involved in every cognitive act. And we can no longer allow ourselves to separate thought from feeling nor to push our subjective experiences into the cognitively irrelevant corner of the emotions (of which poetry, religion, metaphysics, and morality are supposed to be expressions). Knowledge which is at the same time humanistic will then be seen to have a no less legitimate claim than that of any science.

In other words this Series attempts to affirm the truth that man's knowledge can be made relevant to life only by including a knowledge about knowledge. And therefore the humanist can no longer be isolated from the scientist nor can he defend, as he did in the Renaissance, his own studies against the claims of other disciplines. For the humanist even as the scientist has to face the problem of truth, a problem which may be treated in multiple ways, retaining the emphasis, however, on the quest for unity, for that which is constant, in the face of apparently divergent and incompatible doctrines. *Perspectives in Humanism* suggests that one of man's fundamental concerns, be he scientist, philosopher, theologian, artist, or political thinker, is the humanist authority which derives from truth and not the technological authority which derives from power.

Humanism, it is shown here, differs from the specific humanisms of past history in that it forces the mind again and again to recognize wider and subtler relations, lifting seemingly unrelated patterns into a higher harmony. A knowledge of past humanisms is of course indispensable, since some of this knowledge is intrinsically valid and true, and we are summoned to recognize this before we can make significant contributions to our own humanism. This is the heritage each generation is called upon to transmit to the future. It is the humanist heritage which is synonymous with a doctrine of man, explored, enriched, and enlarged for the benefit of mankind and society.

Humanism as presented in this Series affirms the dependence of cultural values on concrete realities. We cannot conceive the former apart from the latter any more than we can conceive a painting apart from its pigment and canvas. And the unity, the constant, in both instances belongs to the realm of values. Therein lie their essence, meaning, and reality. And it is no difficult task to show that those who reject such interpretations in the name of scientific method, of blood, of iron, of property, or of economic necessity, and are therefore scornful of humanism as an ineffective phantasm, are themselves actuated to this scorn by dogmas, ideologies, or other value-impregnated thought forms, which can come to terms with the former only in the eternal arena of humanistic ideas.

The socialist program of humanism as envisaged by the communists has failed, and henceforth we cannot speak of the problem of Man as having significance only after the collapse of capitalism. For to offer man only what is human is to betray him and to wish him ill, since by the principal part of him which is the mind and the heart man is called to something better than a merely historical or physical life. As Aristotle reminds us, "To propose to man a merely human end is to misunderstand nature."

It is clear that whoever uses the term humanism (and the term itself is ambiguous) brings into play at once an entire metaphysic, and the idea we form of humanism will have wholly different implications according to whether we hold or do not hold that there is in the nature of man a constant, an essence, something which breathes an air outside of time and a personality whose profoundest needs transcend time and space, and even the self.

The authors in this Series try to show that humanism is the essence of all disciplines of the human mind. Humanism indeed tends to render man more truly human. It makes man's original greatness manifest itself by causing him to participate in all that can enrich him in nature and in history by concentrating the universe in man and by dilating man to the universe. This Series endeavors to show how, through humanism, man may make use of all the potentialities he holds within him, his creative powers and the life of reason, and how he may make the powers of the physical world the instruments of his freedom.

The question raised by the authors here is: Can humanism become aware of itself and significant to man only in those moments of despair, at a time of the dissipation of its own energies, of isolation, alienation, loss of identity, dissociation, and descent; only when pain opens man's eyes and he sees and finds his burden unendurable? Human, all too human! Does this lead to the proliferation of that atomic anarchy of which Nietzsche has spoken and which Dostoevsky's Grand Inquisitor offers us as a picture of a threatening fate, the nihilism of our time? Is there a humanism conscious of itself and free, leading man to sacrifice and greatness, which is indeed transcendent because here human suffering and consciousness of responsibility open man's eyes? For it is on the humanist answer to this question (and the grounds on which it is decided) that the various positions men take in the face of the travail of history enacted before our eyes and the diverse practical decisions which they feel obliged to make, do in fact depend.

Perspectives in Humanism tries to work toward defining a sound and sane philosophy of modern history so desperately needed. The authors in this Series work to substitute for the inhuman system currently confronting us a new form of civilization which would outline and represent humanism both sacred and secular. *Perspectives in Humanism* tries to show that this humanism is all the more human since it does not worship man but has a real and effective respect for human dignity and for the rights of human personality.

Our age, like every other, is in the grip of its own changing and conflicting thought forms, but the scholar who deals with "facts" cannot achieve objectivity by denuding these "facts" of value, for if he treats them as nonvalues he does not treat them at all. The best he can aspire to is the catholic comprehension and the tolerance that find nothing alien in anything human. Humanism requires that we interpret in our own terms, in the terms of our culture, the total given reality, persistently evaluating it all, means and ends in one, together with the sustaining earth and the indifferent cosmos, and thereby transmuting fact not only into value but also into symbol. This is its necessity, its life, as well as its peril.

The Chinese ideograph, the symbol of humanism, on the jacket and binding of each volume in this Series is found on early Chinese bronzes in the year 1200 B.C. It reflects the vision and image not of an individual man but of all mankind. It is the symbol chosen for the ability of man to transcend his own isolated self, a quality fundamental to his humanity. The "objectivity" of science cannot help man in his present human predicament, since for science in this sense there can be no commitment. So that in the end we know everything but understand nothing. In fact, we would seek nothing, not being motivated by concern for any question. It is a symbol which is concise, not precise; it is reflective, not descriptive. It is the impersonal self, identical from man to man, and is even perhaps similar to the essence of all life in its manifold expressions in nature. This symbol* thereby shows us why, in our search for meaning, direction, historical unities, and experience in science or in life, we must give logical priority as well as metaphysical preeminence to what we call, for lack of a better term, humanism: that which has something in common with intellectual achievement, with moral action, and with love.

* I am indebted and grateful to Professor Chiang Yee, Professor of Art and Calligraphy at Columbia University. He has generously drawn my attention to this ideograph.

R.N.A.

THE LIVING
TRADITION

MOSES
HADAS

CHAPTER 1
PREMISES

If a caterpillar contemplates his future he is presumably reconciled to extinction by the prospect of transformation into a butterfly. Would men be content with the prospect of a posterity in which they could not recognize their own humanity? Before our century is out, we are told, mankind will have undergone an almost total revolution: is this a promise or a threat? How much of familiar humanity can survive into the century following? And if survival is desirable, what can be done to foster it?

History seems reassuring. Revolutions in environment and consequently in outlooks have confronted various peoples with new challenges in the past and compelled them to invent new procedures and adopt new attitudes to make themselves at home in a transformed world. Generally they have been able to absorb changes by adapting existing techniques and usages, often to be sure with alterations more significant than they themselves realized. When a cataclysm has affected a single population others which survived intact have been able in course of time to raise the fallen member or else to close ranks. The stream of culture has sometimes been reduced to a sluggish trickle and sometimes it has made sharp turns and swollen into a torrent, but it has never been wholly interrupted. On the basis of history we should suppose that it would continue into the indefinite future as it derived from the indefinite past.

But now history appears to be an imperfect guide because the dimensions of the revolution, in mass and in scope, are unexampled. Environment will come under control, productivity will be enormously increased, speed of communications will eliminate gradations between advanced and retarded areas, exploration of outer space will reduce international tensions to the level of parochial rivalries. We are approaching the ecumenical ideal in which no isolated group can remain untouched by the fortunes of the whole, with its corollary that the whole may then be homogenized into a consistent level of mediocrity. On the basis of achievements already attained and directions established we might extrapolate a more or less plausible picture of the new world and even of the changes in habits and outlooks it might entail. What makes prophecy most precarious is the potentialities of biological engineering, where the consequences are less predictable. If the mystery of life and the shaping of natural endowments come under control, if the physical and mental constitution of man can be manipulated, what will become of emotions and passions, of poetry and religion, of traditional ideals and aspirations and codes of courtesy?

To envision extinction of such essential expressions of humanity is as difficult as to imagine extinction of self. Every individual knows that he must die and yet continues his habitual activities as long as he is able; he knows that a future existence, if he believes in one, must be utterly revolutionary, and yet he can only picture that existence as agreeable or disagreeable according to gauges appropriate to this world. So we may agree that poetry and ethics and the rest as we know them may disappear, but we can only assume that the impulses and appetites that make these things necessary or desirable are essential ingredients of the genus and are bound to find alternative, if as yet unknown, means of expression. Starkly intellectual speculators impatient of antiquated traditions and vague emotions have suggested that we had better abolish language because of the imprecise connotations with which it is inevitably burdened and communicate with each other through mathematical symbols instead. How long, one wonders, would the symbols remain free of imprecise connotations?

It is revolution, then, not a *tabula rasa*, that we must contemplate, and if recorded history cannot supply a parallel for revolution so far-reaching in technology and so universal in scope, the intellectual and historical experiences of the race may provide bases for speculation upon its problems and perhaps suggestions for their solution. Our first analogy derives from myth rather than history, the familiar myth of Prometheus. When Zeus first came to power and found mankind a cowering and helpless lot he decided to abolish it and replace it with a better race. But Prometheus enabled man to survive by improving his state; he gave him fire and tools, taught him agriculture and navigation, provided him with drugs and the medicine of hope. For primitive man, it might be suggested, fire is a more important and more revolutionary innovation than atomic fission is today, hammer and tongs than all modern technology, agriculture than modern means to abundance, navigation than voyaging into space; and even drugs and hope may adumbrate manipulation of physiology and psychology. From an Olympian point of view Zeus's plan was quite reasonable, and Prometheus was a sentimental do-gooder for meddling with it. But man can only take a human, not an Olympian, view; we cannot be persuaded to efface ourselves, we cannot feel kinship with a butterfly even if it emerges from a chrysalis we ourselves have produced.

The precious thing of which Prometheus and his wards and their posterity to this day have been so tenacious, the one asset they carried from their wretched to their easier state, was of course their humanity. The Prometheus story is a kind of Utopia realized, but all proper utopias, no matter how revolutionary, have been equally tenacious of traditional humanity. We welcome the promise of a revolutionized world in which the flaws and inadequacies of the world we know will be corrected, but even the freest constructions of fancy must find room for the continuing values of humanity which make life in an unredeemed world worth living. That is how the utopias of Thomas More and those of all his predecessors and successors have been constructed. Always the paramount factor which binds the new to the old and gives it plausibility is the persistent tradition of humanity; the good things in Utopia are merely enhancements of desirable tradition, and the reforms are direct repudiations of bad tradition.

Fantasy may freely choose what traditions it will preserve and enhance and what it will revise or reject, but a degree of choice is possible in fact as well as romance because all do not possess the same kind of sanctions. Where a rigorous central authority, political or religious, has been acknowledged, the traditions dictated by official institutions have been binding; that is why utopias regularly envisage reform of the governmental structure, whether in the direction of relaxing or intensifying external authority. But where institutional authority was less exigent, and particularly where it was not reinforced by the sanctions of religion or a quasi-religious mystique, greater concern was shown for what we shall call the traditions of style, which have proved more viable than traditions of external authority. The best illustration of the viability of the tradition of style is that afforded by the history of humanism, and since humanism was invented and transmitted by the Greeks we shall naturally find the Greek experience most instructive. But there have been several historical conjunctures which offer at least partial analogies for our own problem of cultural survival and paradigms for its solution or at least reasonable hope that it can be solved.

The conjunction likeliest to occur to Westerners is that associated with the humanist age following the Renaissance. When the geocentric theory of the universe was supplanted by the heliocentric the firm foundations of the familiar world were shaken and the happy few toppled from their assured position at the crown of creation. When America was discovered horizons were enormously enlarged and the uniqueness of the happy few further diminished. When firearms came into use the dimensions of international relations were revolutionized. When printing presses multiplied books readers too were multiplied and intellectual life more widely shared. It is an exaggeration to say that the impulses which produced these innovations resulted directly from the rediscovery of ancient books; more probably the classics confirmed rather than initiated tendencies already present. But the revived interest in ancient outlooks welded the future to the past, so that the revolution, far-reaching as it was, was not an interruption of the stream of tradition but rather an enlargement of it.

Less familiar but more instructive for our present purposes is a revolution very like that of the humanist age which transformed the ancient world after the conquests of Alexander the Great at the end of the fourth century B.C. The nature of that revolution and its significance we shall discuss in another chapter; here it will suffice to notice that despite the transformed environment and the loss of sovereignty, which in the ancient experience should have entailed the disappearance of the habits and outlooks it is calculated to foster, the Greeks not only maintained their essential Greekhood but succeeded in Hellenizing the Near and Middle East, and then in civilizing Rome, which bequeathed the ancient legacy to the countries of Europe and gave them such cultural unity as they possess to this day. This stunning success the Greeks achieved not through war or diplomacy but by tenacious loyalty to their own style despite the vicissitudes of war and politics.

Speculation about the future of tradition must necessarily take cognizance of its past, and this would properly entail consideration of humanity as far back as we can distinguish it from the animal. But the choice of Greece rather than its predecessors in Anatolia or Egypt or Mesopotamia as a point of departure is not arbitrary. It was in Greece that the contours of European civilization were given shape; it is from the Greeks that we derive our forms of literature and canons of taste, the quest for philosophy, our norms for relationships between man and man and between man and external authority, our democratic ideal. The elements of our culture which derive from the Near East joined the Greek stream after it was constituted, mainly during the Hellenistic revolution. Classical Greece presents a paradoxical combination of freshness and maturity. It is as if the Greeks had come into the world with no ancestors and had attained sophisticated adulthood at a single bound without traversing the spiritual and psychological ailments of infancy and adolescence. Actually, probing beneath the brilliant surface reveals stages of the primitive; like others, Greek civilization was the product of long evolution, fructified by influences from without; the stages of growth and the external influences can now be traced with increasing assurance. But whereas the peoples from whom the Greeks learned, and to a degree those whom they taught, accepted tradition imposed by external authority, Greek outlooks seem to be self-generated, and tradition was subject to constant questioning. Man himself was the arbiter of his outlooks and codes of conduct.

It is the primacy of man which is the essential mark of humanism and the essential ingredient in the humanistic tradition. Corollary to this essential principle and manifestations of it are attitudes to the supernatural, to intractable nature and variable convention, the philosophic enterprise, the conception of the unity of humanity, and the conviction that participation in the humanistic tradition is determined by intelligence and education, not by geography or race. We shall deal first with the principle and some of its manifestations, and then follow the subsequent fortunes of the tradition. Changes in the political and social environment which might have threatened its survival during the Hellenistic Age actually gave it much wider scope, and though the tradition underwent certain alterations its essentials stood fast. It stood fast, again with alterations, through the hegemony of Rome, which transmitted it to the countries of Europe. After a period of somnolence it was reinvigorated in the humanist age; as a paradigm for our current crisis the experience of the humanist age is particularly instructive because its catalyst was a dramatic advance in scientific sophistication. One after another the great writers of the humanist age seem to be resuming the humanistic dialogue of the Greeks where it had been interrupted at the end of antiquity, and it has continued with unabated vigor to this day. It has survived its crises in the past because men have found it illuminating and liberating, but it has had official guardians also, whose function will be glanced at. The tradition itself has practical utility for traversing revolutionary changes induced by scientific progress and alterations in the political and social structure, but its greatest use is in safeguarding individuality against the threat of homogenization and regimentation. How this potentiality may be realized will be the subject of the concluding chapters.

CHAPTER 2

MAN
THE
MEASURE

The salient distinction of the Greek outlook upon the world is that it is anthropocentric. It is this which is the essence of the humanist code, this which distinguishes the Greeks from their predecessors and rivals, and this which is ultimately responsible for their extraordinary cultural achievements and their democracy. The essence of the code was formulated in the famous dictum of the Sophist Protagoras about the middle of the fifth century B.C.: "Man is the measure of all things." But it is operative throughout the course of Greek experience. It is adumbrated in Homer, at the far end of Greek literature, and given a philosophic rationale by the Epicureans, at the near end, and it is basic to almost everything that comes between. This is not to say that it was the sole or orthodox position ("orthodoxy" is anyhow irrelevant where there is no revelation or established religion), or for long stretches of time and among large segments of the population the dominant view. In fact, the doctrine and its adherents were strenuously opposed by such respectable authorities as Aristophanes and Plato. In retrospect, nevertheless, the doctrine of man the measure may well be regarded as the most characteristic and most seminal of all Greek contributions to civilization, and of particular importance to our present theme.

It is easy to see why the doctrine must have been abhorrent to men who favored otherworldly religion or conservative politics for it was potentially subversive of all institutions and usages and all authority. Unless acknowledged external authority is posited for the establishment and continuance of traditional institutions they must be conceived of as the creations of men, to meet men's emergent needs. Their only sanction is expediency, and they must be continually reexamined for their validity; when they cease to be expedient, institutional traditions may be disregarded, calmly and without rebelliousness. Traditions of proper individual deportment and artistic expression, on the other hand, are on a different footing. Though these too have been created and elaborated by men they are more exigent because they constitute the substance of civilization, which would be reduced to barbarism if its traditions were abandoned. But even in conduct moral injunctions are relative; depending on circumstances a man may be guilty of the crime of *hybris*, for example, merely by failing to rise before an elder, or he may use physical violence without committing *hybris*.

For people who assign the measure of man to external powers and standards the assumption of authority by man himself seems arrogant and impious. This view of the Sophists' impiety they find confirmed in another dictum of Protagoras: "Of the gods I do not speak because I cannot know." Actually this second dictum, which is the logical justification of the first, may be construed as an expression of pure and humble piety. In the absence of revelation, who *can* speak with assurance about the gods? Are not those who do so, like Job's friends, the arrogant ones, gauging God by their own human standards? There have been sects in several religions which condemned any predication concerning deity, favorable or otherwise, as blasphemous, because any predication puts the speaker in the position of passing judgment upon the divine and therefore by implication of regarding himself as the superior. So far from implying derogation, the profession of ignorance may suggest an uncommonly lofty theology.

It is not then that the gods are denied or scorned. It is rather that they occupy a different sphere from the human and practice a different kind of mathematics. They lead their own immortal lives, and their principal occupation is not, as it seems to be for monotheists, to set a pattern for and regulate the lives of mortals and to reckon rewards and punishments for observing the pattern or transgressing it. If the gods make two and two equal five man cannot fault them but must not imitate them. Rather he must continue to observe correct human arithmetic, he must behave well as man. If, behaving well as man, he is tripped up by forces beyond his control we have tragedy. It is of the greatest importance to observe that tragic suffering is not viewed as condign punishment (though generations of readers have so interpreted it) but rather, as we shall presently see, as confirmation of the victim's own heroic quality. A man becomes a hero not by bowing to tradition but by transcending it.

Proper assessment of a people's ethical and moral outlooks and deportment must depend on an understanding of their religious views: what do their gods require of them, and how exigent are these requirements? But understanding the religious views of the Greeks requires effort, for we tend to regard religion as a constant and assume that definitions which two millennia of a different tradition have made second nature to us are equally applicable to the Greeks. Whatever our private beliefs may be, for us religion means monotheism, a preoccupation with theology, a series of moral imperatives. The Greeks were polytheists, concerned with cult rather than theology, and tended to base conduct rather on secular sanctions than on religious prescriptions. Divinity did not reside in a single omnipotent and benevolent deity; there were many gods, in several categories, and none was particularly benevolent, or, what is more important for our purpose, omnipotent. Each had his own predilections; what one god might approve another might condemn, and since both had power to punish it was the individual human who had to choose the one—and accept punishment at the hands of the other. Man himself is the arbiter. There was nothing like an official list of injunctions and prohibitions with a fixed tariff of pains and penalties. Even for murder retribution was originally the responsibility of the victim's kin; the state became concerned only because blood unavenged creates a public pollution which must be cleansed.

Over all the gods including Zeus himself (though here there is some ambiguity) was the overriding power of fate. As every reader of Homer knew, Zeus could not save his own son from his fated death, could not resist the charms of a series of mortal women (whom he is represented as listing in *Iliad* 14) nor the seductions of Hera who could henpeck him or seduce him from his proper business. Aphrodite and Ares are represented in an adulterous embrace (in *Odyssey* 8) and are caught and punished. No such gods could be taken seriously as establishing a tradition for men to emulate. As far back as the sixth century B.C., Xenophanes complained that Homer and Hesiod attributed to the gods everything that is disgraceful and blameworthy among men, theft and adultery and mutual deceit. "If oxen and lions had hands to draw and make things as men do," Xenophanes said, "they would draw the shapes of their gods and fashion their bodies like the forms they themselves have, horses like horses and oxen like oxen."

The first impression of a casual reader of Greek literature confirms the Shakespearean line: "As flies to wanton boys, are we to the gods." Men would fare better without them; the gods are responsible for most human afflictions and do little to relieve them. Advanced thinkers like Euripides might murmur that gods who behave outrageously do not deserve their status, but not even Euripides, as we shall presently see, denied that they possessed it. The crucial point is that their status was not predicated on the perfection and finality which is associated with monotheism. Men must frame their own programs independently of the gods or even in opposition to them and not suppress their own counsels in favor of a dubious tradition.

Our fullest and most trustworthy informants on the religious climate of fifth-century Athens are the tragic poets, who occupied a place analogous to that of Old Testament prophets. They were regarded and regarded themselves as teachers, their plays were produced under state auspices and exhibited to very large audiences, and their merits were gauged in public competitions by representatives of the audience, so that they cannot be suspected of deviating too widely from the general sense of the community. They are thus more trustworthy spokesmen than the professed philosophers, who might tower high above the generality, or than lyric poets, who might express private caprices.

Of the three tragic poets whose work has survived (portions of it, that is) the one who comes closest to our sense of religion and who is most deeply concerned to justify the ways of gods to men is Aeschylus. One remarkable passage (*Suppliants* 90–104) might have been uttered by an Old Testament prophet:

> Secure it falls upon its feet, not upon its back,
> whatever thing is decreed to fulfillment by
>   Zeus's nod;
> through thicket and shadow stretch the paths
>   of his understanding
> and no speculation can spy them out.
> From the high towers of their hopes he hurls
>   men to utter ruin,
> yet no armed violence need he array;
> all that is divine is effortless.
> From the holy throne where he is firmly seated,
> somehow he carries his thought into deed.

Another passage in the same play (590–599) reads:

> To whom of the gods could I more fitly appeal?
> Thou, Lord, art our father, thine own hand
>   has planted us,

thou art the ancient artificer of our race,
thou Zeus whose breath prospereth all things.
He sits not upon his throne 'neath another's
    suzerainty,
no humbler dominion does he hold 'neath a
    mightier power,
he honors no sovereignty of higher seat;
with him the deed is as the word,
swiftly to execute what his counseling mind
    brings forth.

And yet despite the omnipotence apparently attributed to Zeus, responsibility for moral choice is still man's. Of his plays, the *Suppliants* and the trilogy called *Oresteia* show a conflict of principle between the more primitive chthonic deities and the more advanced Olympians, of which the up-shot is that man himself is the proper arbiter. In the *Suppliants* a good and conscientious king is suddenly confronted, through no fault of his own, by fifty maidens who are flying from marriage with their Egyptian cousins and who sue for asylum. According to the chthonic principle of the primacy of blood, bonds of kinship (which the girls can claim) would entitle them to asylum; but to grant asylum might precipitate war with a powerful foreign enemy, and would therefore be contrary to Apollo's principle of orderly government. Each sanction has its own validity; the responsibility for choice is man's. How the opposing claims were eventually reconciled we can only surmise, for the conclusion of the trilogy has not survived. In the *Oresteia*, which has survived complete, we are told. Here Orestes is directed by Apollo to avenge the death of his father Agamemnon; the murder of a king by a woman is a monstrous violation of order and must be punished. But to avenge his father Orestes must kill his mother—the most abhorrent of all crimes in the chthonian view. The Furies who persecute Orestes are not evil witches but legitimate prosecutors of the murder of kin in the old order. The denouement in the *Eumenides*, the concluding play of the trilogy, shows the triumph of humanism. The Furies' mechanical principle of blood for blood is abolished (the Furies themselves are given more enlightened duties), and instead the system of trial by jury is established. A man is not to be condemned by a hoary tradition but is to be judged, with proper consideration of circumstances and degrees of guilt, by his own peers. Man is the measure of all things, even for the devout Aeschylus.

Not only as between two orders of deities but in conflicting principles among the Olympians also man is the measure. Hippolytus, in Euripides' play of that name, has devoted himself to the chaste outdoor goddess Artemis and scorns the works of Aphrodite. To avenge this affront Aphrodite causes Hippolytus's death; all Artemis can do for her devotee is to assure him that she will one day ruin some protégé of Aphrodite's—an odd example of divine justice, inferior not only to European ethical standards but, as Euripides' audience must surely have recognized, to current Greek ones. It is not that Hippolytus chose badly; as Artemis's promise shows, if he had followed Aphrodite's way instead of hers Artemis would have worked his destruction. Euripides' *Bacchae* shows a similar conflict, between Apollo and Dionysus. King Pentheus chooses to cleave to Apollonian rationality and orderliness and rejects Dionysus and the principle of release for which he stands. There is some logic in Dionysus' doing him to death, and we cannot expect Apollo to intervene; but why should Dionysus compel Agave, who had accepted him, to decapitate her own son? Human sensibilities are offended by such wanton cruelty, and no less in Euripides' day than in ours. Clearly the gods do not provide models for emulation; men can be expected to work out their own moral codes.

The behavior of the gods in these instances may appear less offensive if we conceive of them not as concerned with total personality but as presiding severally over disparate emotions and impulses. If monotheism is a synthesis of various divine activities, polytheism is an analysis, assigning separate functions to specific deities. If Aphrodite typifies the realm of sexual love then to reject her is to abdicate an important area of humanity, to commit partial suicide, as it were, which is indeed a fatal marring of human life. To reject the Dionysiac element of life, exuberance and enthusiasm and release, is equally fatal. And so it would impoverish a man's life and diminish his humanity if he resigned from Artemis's realm of outdoor life and animal creation, or from that of Hermes, who is the patron of poets and traders and cunning contrivers.

Even in Homer the normal mode of divine intervention on behalf of mortals is not by interposing a miracle, that is, an interruption of the ordinary course of nature, but by causing the individual to use his own human intelligence and strength at their highest effectiveness. Near the beginning of the *Iliad,* Achilles half-draws his sword from its scabbard to attack Agamemnon in open meeting. Athena (whom no man besides sees) does not grasp his wrist but merely gives him a blazing look—and Achilles himself decides that there are more fitting ways to deal with Agamemnon and returns his sword to its scabbard. This mode of intervention is quite regular in Homer. On the rare occasions when the gods help rather than hinder, what is expected of them is not an eclipse or transformation of humanity but an intensification of it. A popular Greek story crystallizes the principle. A man whose cart was mired called upon mighty Heracles for help, and when Heracles appeared, prepared to sit down and wait for results. "Not that way," said Heracles. "Put your shoulder to the wheel." Whatever the gods might do, man must put forth his own best effort; the responsibility is his.

Where gods occupied a different sphere from the human and practiced a different mathematics, heroes were mortals, different in degree from other men but not in kind. Hence they were closer to ordinary activities and outlooks and closer too to men's minds and hearts. Attitudes to heroes and heroization therefore afford an excellent insight into Greek humanism. In its proper Greek sense "hero" does not signify merely the principal personage in a work of literature or, except metaphorically, any champion of out-standing prowess. A hero is a man now dead whose career in life had been so extraordinary as to enlarge the horizons of what is possible for man, in consequence of which he receives a cult. This means that offerings of wine or flowers might be made on stated days at his shrine or *heroon* (which need be only a stock or a stone; *heroa* were very numerous, in city and countryside) and that his name might be invoked in activities like his own. The institution is analogous to that of saints, who also receive a cult after death in recognition of an extraordinary career in life. But whereas the saint rises to an ideal above ordinary human-ity, the hero emphasizes the potentialities of the human; indeed he is often so obsessed with self-interest as to fall below ordinary norms of conduct. Often he proves a prickly companion and a bad citizen. Achilles himself, the beau ideal of heroism, was such a man. Because he is ob-sessed with his own glory he is insubordinate to authority and indifferent to the desperate need of his comrades. He may be chided for hardheartedness but no one ever com-plains that he is violating traditional norms. On the con-trary, as we shall see in another chapter, he becomes the paradigm for transcending tradition.

Sophocles was called the most Homeric of the tragedians, doubtless because his personages preserve the Homeric spa-ciousness and the heroic norms and are not deflated to the level of the commonplace as they are in Euripides. Where Euripides depicted men as they are, Sophocles is reported to have said, he himself painted them as they should be; and it is instructive to see what Sophocles thought a good man should be like. Almost all of his plays amount to a demonstration that a personage accepted as a hero did in fact deserve that status, that his failings were the necessary obverse of his merits, and that his eventual fall is not a con-demnation of his career but on the contrary an affirmation of his heroism.

Consider Sophocles' earliest extant play, the *Ajax*. This is what we know of its hero. First, he was self-willed and independent: at the beginning of his career when he was advised to pray to the gods for success, he asserted that he could win success without their help, and when darkness fell during a battle he prayed not for help in fighting but only for light to fight by. He was an unsubtle man: when Achilles rejected Agamemnon's offer of atonement for taking Briseis, Ajax could not understand why seven women are not preferable to one—we remember Shakespeare's "beef-witted lord." He was very strong: in the absence of Achilles he was the only Greek who could stem the Trojan rush to burn the ships. He was proud: where Hector prayed that his son might surpass him, the limit of Ajax's prayer was that his son might equal him. When the weapons of slain Achilles, which were to go "to the best of the Greeks," were awarded to Odysseus instead of to himself, Ajax was so affronted that he would have assassinated the generals if Athena had not confounded his wits, so that he slaughtered the army's cattle instead. At the opening of the play, before he recovers his wits, Athena herself condemns his pride and insubordination and foretells his fall. In the play he exhibits brutal unconcern for his wife and crew, who are wholly dependent on him for safety, and then commits suicide. Agamemnon and Menelaus forbid burial; organized society cannot subsist if self-willed recalcitrants like Ajax are not dishonored. Odysseus persuades them to relent; and the burial which Ajax receives is tantamount to an approval of the totality of his career. A man cannot be split in two; if we want one who can stop an enemy army single-handed we cannot expect a namby-pamby but must take truculence and even brutality into the bargain. Individual will and individual achievement can transcend not only the constituted authorities of society but even the expressed pronouncement of the goddess Athena.

Antigone also shows flouting of constituted authority, but this time on the plea of the higher sanction of "unwritten law." But to accept this plea as valid and hence to regard Antigone as a pagan saint may be a modern error. To the Greek audience Creon's ban against burying Polyneices must have seemed right; how could a conscientious magistrate honor the traitor who came to destroy his city equally with its savior? On the other hand, Antigone's passion is abnormal, as she shows in her speeches, especially to the normal Ismene, and in her *second* burial of Polyneices. It is made clear that the burial was not earth-to-earth but merely a ritual casting on of dust; why then need it have been repeated, except to show Antigone's abnormality? An unwritten law is what one chooses to make it and relates rather to "style" (which we shall deal with in another chapter) than to acknowledged jurisprudence. If then Creon is right and is brought to ruin, and Antigone is wrong and receives the martyrdom she seems to crave, why is the play not named for Creon? Because a girl who surrenders love and life itself for what she conceives is right does enlarge human horizons and so is worthy of heroization, and we cannot expect that a normal girl would act so, just as we could not expect that a normal man should show the prowess of Ajax. What we gather from *Antigone* is not so much piety to higher authority as a free approach to all authority.

Oedipus the King in particular has been subject to pious misinterpretation as a moral tableau demonstrating inescapable retribution for crime. But can a thoughtful modern or could a thoughtful ancient regard the punishment visited on Oedipus as just? The crimes had been predestined and it was impossible for him to avoid them, though he tried hard to do so. On the other hand, he persisted in his search for the truth after it had become evident that the quest would be dangerous to himself. He was indeed hasty in temper and suspicious of friends who meant him well, but without these faults he would not have been the man to pursue his quest so relentlessly. If there was a guilty party it was not Oedipus but Apollo; but Apollo, as we have seen, is above human arithmetic. As a man Oedipus behaved well, and his fall is not a token of disapproval or defeat but a victorious affirmation of his heroism. It is the man who behaves singularly well and who ventures freely to assert his humanity who is liable to be tripped up by forces outside his control and so become the subject of tragedy. His fall is not a warning but an example.

The merit of each of these heroes is accompanied by a defect—Ajax's brutality, Antigone's abnormality, Oedipus's impatient temper—and these have been regarded as "tragic flaws" which justify the disaster visited upon the tragic victim. Perfectionist systems of morality, as for example early Stoicism, do not recognize degrees of wrongdoing; a miss is as good as a mile and a man drowned in three inches of water is as dead as a man drowned in three fathoms. But only doctrinaires can equate misdemeanors and felonies; reasonable men and reasonable systems of law draw a distinction between jaywalking and armed robbery. If the eventual disaster is said to be justified by a tragic flaw it is not a balance of weights, making the punishment fit the crime, but rather in the nature of a placebo for the audience. To represent the fall of a perfect character is, as Aristotle says, shocking, and it may ease the shock to show the fallen man as having been less than perfect. But who *is* perfect? None of the heroes of tragedy, and no man of sufficient stature to become a hero of tragedy. Tragic flaw is not a reproach but a description. The world we deal with is a world of men, and we do not expect or wish men to discard their humanity, nor even reproach them when their assertion of individuality proves inconvenient to ourselves.

Heroes are salutary for the community not because their aim is to serve the common interest but because they strive for individual excellence, which then works to the advantage of the community. Individual interest and glory, not the abstraction of patriotism, is the motivation of the warrior. The battle songs composed by Callinus and Tyrtaeus in the seventh century B.C. invoke no such abstractions: it is advisable for men to stand shoulder to shoulder and fight stoutly, they say, in order to prevent their lands from being taken away and their wives from being enslaved. The cardinal sin of the disciplined warrior was to lose his shield: "Either with this or on it," the Spartan mother is reported to have said when she sent her son to war. For cogent personal reasons Archilochus not only threw his shield away but then compounded the dereliction in a poem:

> Some Thracian strutteth with my shield;
> For, being somewhat flurried,
> I left it in a wayside bush,
> When from the field I hurried;
> A right good targe but I got off,
> The deuce may take the shield;
> I'll get another just as good
> When next I go afield.
>
> (*Translated by* PAUL SHOREY)

Individual reason, not traditional rule, is the motive for action.

Permissiveness for deviations from what we should regard as absolutes is manifested not only in literary figures and creations but also in historical personages. Accusations of bribery were very common, and seem to have brought the culprit no permanent disgrace. Even treason could be digested. The greatest military victory of the Greeks was that over the Persian invaders at the beginning of the fifth century; this victory secured the freedom of Greece and initiated its golden age of political and cultural achievement. The great architect of the victory was Themistocles. His services were duly recognized, but then he was charged with some malfeasance, and went over to the Persian king to take service with a power which was a continuing threat to Greece. Athenians were naturally irked, but no one cried treason. A man was entitled to take due regard to his own interests and personality; many must have reflected that they would have behaved similarly in similar circumstances. The Spartan Pausanias and, during the Pelopon-

nesian War, the Athenian Alcibiades did do as Themistocles had done. And despite the grievous injury Alcibiades
had done his city, Athens was willing to avail itself of his
services again later in the war.

It was not morally shocking, then, for Socrates' respectable friends to advise him to escape when he was awaiting
execution in 399 B.C. In rejecting his friends' proffered
help, according to Plato's accounts, Socrates does not invoke an abstract principle of patriotism but cites the practical advantages he had received from the laws of the city
which he must now requite: they had formed and sheltered
him, and in return he must keep the post they had assigned
him. It is hard to imagine that many of Socrates' own disciples would have shown such selfless punctilio. One of them,
indeed, the pedestrian Xenophon, who deals with the offer
of Socrates' friends in his own version of the *Apology of
Socrates,* makes no mention of the argument of obligation:
Socrates rejected his friends' offer to help him escape simply because he was old and tired and wished to be done with
life. The sum of the matter is that individual reason, not
tradition, is the motive for conduct.

And man is responsible for his achievements also. Where
Aeschylus's Prometheus had boasted that he had bestowed
upon man the arts that made life possible, Sophocles asserts
that it is by man's own resourcefulness and ingenuity that
he has learned navigation and agriculture, hunting and do-
mesticating animals, speech and thought and protection
against weather. Here is the famous choral ode on the wonders of man in Sophocles' *Antigone:*

Wonders are many, and none is more wonderful than man;
the power that crosses the white sea, driven by the stormy
south-wind, making a path under surges that threaten to en-
gulf him; and Earth, the eldest of the gods, the immortal, the
unwearied, doth he wear, turning the soil with the offspring of
horses, as the ploughs go to and fro from year to year.
And the light-hearted race of birds, and the tribes of savage

beasts, and the sea-brood of the deep, he snares in the meshes of his woven toils, he leads captive, man excellent in wit. And he masters by his arts the beast whose lair is in the wilds, who roams the hills; he tames the horse of shaggy mane, he puts the yoke upon its neck, he tames the tireless mountain bull.

And speech, and wind-swift thought, and all the moods that mould a state, hath he taught himself; and how to flee the arrows of the frost, when 'tis hard lodging under the clear sky, and the arrows of the rushing rain; yea, he hath resource for all; without resource he meets nothing that must come; only against Death shall he call for aid in vain; but from baffling maladies he hath devised escapes.

Cunning beyond fancy's dream is the fertile skill which brings him, now to evil, now to good. When he honours the laws of the land, and that justice which he hath sworn by the gods to uphold, proudly stands his city; no city hath he who, for his rashness, dwells with sin. Never may he share my hearth, never think my thoughts, who doth these things!

(*Translated by* R. C. JEBB)

The concluding strophe is a warning that man should not apply his resourcefulness and ingenuity to disregard the laws of the city. But even here the choice is man's own; Antigone becomes a heroine precisely because she does disregard the law of the city.

Where the measure of man is some external power the individual may find fulfillment by willing subordination to it and be content with anonymity. But where man is the measure, men fulfill themselves by the assertion of their individuality and the witness of public notice. Meekness was never a virtue among the Greeks, and they were never reticent about their pursuit and achievement of excellence. At all periods the drive towards personal distinction was considered not only legitimate but praiseworthy, and this drive may well be ultimately responsible not only for democracy but also for extraordinary attainments in arts and letters.

As for other Greek outlooks, the pattern is provided by Homer. Achilles' overriding passion, and the chief motivation for his extraordinary prowess, is for glory; his program is accepted without question as taking precedence over loyalty to commanders and consideration for comrades. A Homeric father sending his son out into the world admonishes him, "Always be the best, always be above all others." The unheroic Hesiod holds out public esteem as a motive for accumulating wealth. "All we men of mortal mold," says Solon, "good alike and bad, think by straining every nerve to win a fair name, each for himself, by his own unaided efforts." "May I have neither gold in my house nor skill to sing a sweeter song than Orpheus if my fortune is to be hid from the eyes of men" is a sentiment by no means peculiar to the tragic hero who uttered it. In an unheroic age Isocrates says (*Evagoras* 3): "We shall find that ambitious and high-souled men . . . choose a glorious death in preference to life and are more jealous of their reputations than of their existence, shrinking from nothing in order to leave behind a remembrance of themselves that shall never die." And in Plato's *Symposium* Socrates quotes Diotima as saying: "Think only of the ambition of men and you will wonder at the senselessness of their ways, unless you consider how they are stirred by the love of an immortality of fame. They are ready to run all risks, greater far than they would have run for their children, and to spend money and undergo any sort of toil, and even to die, for the sake of leaving behind them a name that shall be eternal."

Obsession with fame was not peculiar to warriors and statesmen; the "agonistic" or competitive element permeated all aspects of life. A playwright composed a drama not as the spirit moved him but as an entry in an organized dramatic competition, with a view to winning a prize, and the greatest prize of all was commemoration of his name on a public monument. Potters and painters, both of costly artistic vases and of ordinary household ware, took pains to sign their work. Signatures are so characteristic an index of humanism that they constitute a convenient gauge for its vitality; at the end of antiquity they disappear into anonymity, and then receive renewed emphasis when humanism recovers its vitality.

If men yearned to become the subject of song for generations to come, they yearned even more to be commemorated in stone; this explains the frequent occurrence of statues of Greek athletes. In general the human figure occupies a more prominent place in Greek than in other art, and its anatomy is studied much more carefully than, for example, in the highly sophisticated art of the Far East. Man is truly the measure; the Greeks would surely have been puzzled by a nonrepresentational art divorced from humanity. The archaic *kouroi* show an interesting advance over the Egyptian models which were doubtless their inspiration: one foot is placed forward, to show that the body functions, and the "archaic grin" shows that the mind functions also. Man is the measure, but man with his faculties alert.

The fair coin has its obverse. If good competition produces better bards and better potters, as Hesiod says, bad competition produces strife. We can see its effects in the jealous particularism of the tiny Greek city-states, which kept them at almost constant war with one another and prevented common action which might be salutary to all. It can hardly be accident that the revitalized obsession with the individual in the humanist age was followed by intensification of national consciousnesses which had been the bane of Europe. But along with their stress upon individualism the Greeks also adumbrated the ecumenical ideal, as we shall see in a subsequent chapter, and during the Hellenistic Age showed that coexistence of individualism and the ecumenical ideal was not only possible but fruitful. In our own humanism the importance of the individual is axiomatic, and, current appearances to the contrary notwithstanding, the ecumenical ideal is nearer realization than ever before. Again the obverse will be transcended.

CHAPTER 3
NATURE AND CONVENTION

But not everything in the world will yield to human will; some forces are what they are "by nature" and therefore intractable. To these man can only accommodate himself, but things that are what they are by convention were instituted by men to meet some current need, and when their usefulness is over they may and should be abolished or changed. Tradition tends to assign an origin "in nature" to things whose origin is really "in convention" in order to endow certain institutions and usages with absolute validity; the rational man will differentiate carefully between the two kinds of sanction, and be ready to abandon institutions and usages whose only sanction is tradition when they have lost the expediency for which they were established. Like the doctrine of man the measure, the dichotomy of nature and convention, which is its corollary, can be discerned in all periods of Greek literature, and like the formulation of man the measure it too was crystallized by Sophist teachers in the middle of the fifth century B.C.

Differences among human beings which are likeliest to be attributed to "nature" are those associated with distinctions of race; especially is "difference in nature" invoked when one race regards itself as an elect. The Greeks were not coy about their own merits, but they never thought they were molded out of finer clay than other men. From

Homer and the pre-Socratics onwards, as we shall see in another chapter, they believed in the unity of mankind, and their discussions of political theory or ethics presuppose a uniform human nature, not a specific Greek nature. The rationale for this belief, adumbrated in Homer and made explicit in the pre-Socratics, is biological and physiological; because their bodies operate alike men must belong to a single species. If men are to be sorted into classes, the proper criterion is not race but intelligence. The conception of the distinction between "nature" and "convention" is implicit in the earliest writers, and sometimes the two words are actually contrasted; but its basis in biology was crystallized most sharply by Hippocrates, the medical scientist on the island of Cos. In his treatise *On Air, Earth, Waters* (we should say *On Climate*) he suggested that differences between peoples of various regions and appearances are only superficial and due to environmental differences, and that all men really belong to a single species. Variations in food or language, pigmentation, form of hair and features, are shaped by particular conditions and not essential. Elsewhere in the Hippocratic corpus the distinction between *nomos* (convention or law) and *physis* (nature) is made more specific. In *On Nurture* (1.11) we read: "*Nomos* men make for themselves, without knowing the things about which they legislate: but the *physis* of everything is ordained by the gods. What men legislate never abides the same, whether it is right or wrong; what the gods ordain always abides upright, whether it is right or wrong. That is the difference."

Hippocrates was interested only in his scientific observation, but it was his logic, apparently, that was exploited by the Sophists to promote social reform. A famous papyrus fragment of the Sophist Antiphon (to be distinguished from the well-known orator of the same name) demonstrates the universality of *physis* by the argument that Hellenes and barbarians breathe alike through nostrils and mouth and take their food alike (Diels-Kranz 44A, 2.353). The distinction between them is not in physiology but must be the result of artificial evolution. Not only are discriminations between Greek and foreigner without basis in nature but so also, then, are distinctions between noble and commoner, the privileged and the humble, men and women, the illegitimate and the trueborn. All of these were created by men because they were advantageous. But there is no reason for a woman, say, to remain satisfied with an inferior status simply because such a status was found expedient for women in her grandmother's day. And not only would the validity of class distinctions need to be scrutinized, but various institutions, political or religious, would have to be reexamined daily and disregarded if found no longer serviceable. Denying validity to tradition in society and politics and religion must be anathema to conservatives, and since the writers who figure most prominently in surviving Greek literature happen to have been conservatives it is little wonder that "Sophist" has acquired the odious connotations it still bears. But their very animus shows that Sophist reasoning was creating a ferment, and we can detect traces of it not only in Plato and Aristophanes but also in Thucydides and Euripides.

In the opening pages of Plato's *Republic* where definitions of justice are being canvassed, Thrasymachus offers the "natural" view of the Sophists that justice is the right of the stronger. Such monstrous morality must be refuted by Socrates, and Thrasymachus can only sneer that Socrates needs a nurse to keep his nose wiped. But though Thrasymachus's definition is dismissed and does not reappear in the remainder of the *Republic*, in Thucydides, who wrote nearly a generation before, the same position is taken by the Athenians in justifying the morally questionable acquisition of an empire and again in justifying their savagery to the Melians for choosing to remain aloof from that empire. At the congress held at Lacedaemon before overt hostilities began the Athenians are reported to have said (1.76): "It was not remarkable nor contrary to normal human behavior if we did accept an empire offered to us and refused to give it up, under pressure of the three strongest motives— fear, interest, and honor. It was not we who initiated such conduct, for it has always been natural that the weaker should be subject to the stronger." And to the Melians, in the seventeenth year of the war (5.90 ff.): "Right, as the world goes, is only in question between equals in power; the strong do what they can and the weak suffer what they must." And when, barred from arguments of human morality, the Melians cite the probable displeasure of the gods, the Athenians reply: "Of the gods we believe, and of men we know, that by a necessary law of their nature they rule wherever they can; and it is not as if we were the first to make this law or to act upon it when made; we found it existing before us, and shall leave it to exist forever after us; all that we do is to make use of it, knowing that you and everybody else, having the same power we have, would do the same as we do." At least the Athenians did not resort to hypocrisy and claim, as later imperial powers have felt constrained to do, that their motives were philanthropic. Actually, as Thucydides concludes the episode, after strenuous resistance "the Melians surrendered at discretion to the Athenians, who put to death all the grown men whom they took, and sold the women and children for slaves." Thucydides was not the only Athenian to be shocked by this inhumanity. Euripides, who had glorified Athenian chivalry at the opening of the war in his *Andromache,* was moved to write the *Trojan Women,* which promises requital for those who trample sanctities.

Aristophanes' principal attack upon Sophist notions is his *Clouds.* The claim proffered by the spokesmen of the Sophists (who were also teachers of eloquence) that they could "make the worse appear the better cause" is tantamount to a denial of morality. (But "worse" and "better" in Greek can also mean "weaker" and "stronger," and it may be a work of righteousness to strengthen a good case which appears weak.) Throughout the disputation between Right Logic and Wrong Logic, the former maintains the force of tradition and the latter derides it. For example:

> The Lesser Logic am I? Your sages call me so
> Because the pioneer was I in devising refutations
> Of laws that on conventions rest and codified traditions.

When the new graduate in Sophist doctrine offers to beat his father, the old man protests:

> But nowhere does the law provide that fathers should
> be so treated.

And the son replies:

> Was he more than mortal, of different clay, who that
> law legislated?
> Have we not the same good right by *persuasion* to
> innovate;
> To allow sons who have beaten been on their sires to
> retaliate?
> For old-law whippings we have got a moratorium we'll
> declare.
> Consider roosters and other beasts—do they their
> fathers spare?
> How do such creatures differ from us except that they
> write no decrees?

The father finds the argument irresistible, but loses patience when the son proposes to beat his mother also, and proceeds to burn down the "Thinkery" where such subversive doctrine was taught. But rationalists could scarcely be convinced that the burning of a school was a sufficiently philosophical refutation of the doctrines taught there.

The social reforms implicit in the nature/convention dichotomy are most accessible in the plays of Euripides; a number of them are in effect pamphlets in favor of such reforms. First of all, Euripides makes a conscious effort to discredit the outworn ideals and outlooks of heroic legend. His method is simple. He employs the old plots and dramatis personae, as the usage of the Athenian stage required, but the great names are now borne by contemporary types, sometimes shabbily dressed, living in a contemporary world, and actions which had been glorified by tradition are seen as contemptible and immoral and mad. All of the plots drawn from the Argive cycle show this approach; it is particularly striking in the case of the *Electra* because here we have the exalted parallels in plays of Aeschylus and Sophocles for comparison. We now see Orestes as a timid ruffian, Electra as a psychotic slattern, Clytemnestra as a domestic suburbanite, Aegisthus as an amiable host, and the murders as repulsively cruel and meaningless. Traditional legend is not simply neutral, to be taken or left; it is positively harmful in obfuscating reality and inculcating misleading and harmful standards of behavior.

Other of Euripides' plays show the undesirable consequences of disabilities imposed by sex or status which are assumed to be natural but are in fact only conventional. In *Alcestis* a courteous and otherwise sensitive man can assume that a man's life is so much more valuable than a woman's that it is proper for her to take his place in death. The audience was doubtless in full agreement with this position, at least initially; possibly the progress of the play moved some of them to reconsider. So in the *Medea* Jason's treatment of Medea is posited upon an unquestioned assumption that woman is inferior to man, plus another shared by the audience, that foreigners are inferior to Greeks. If Medea had been respected as a man and a Greek would have been, there need have been no tragedy. And if Hippolytus had not been oppressed by his taint of bastardy he would not have reacted so violently against the works of Aphrodite. The depressed status of bastards, foreigners, women, is after all based not on nature but on convention, and as such is subject to revision. During his lifetime Euripides won very few firsts in the tragic competitions; the fact that his vogue increased after his death may suggest that his views found increasing favor.

We can surmise that the dichotomy between nature and convention was widely acknowledged because men who were opposed to Sophist teaching were forced to take cognizance of it. Sophocles was impatient with Euripides' realism, and said that he himself painted men as they should be rather than as they are. In *Oedipus the King,* written in Sophocles' prime, Oedipus readily acknowledges that he has been proved vile; in *Oedipus at Colonus,* written at the end of Sophocles' life, the blind and old Oedipus has learned to protest: "But in *nature* how was I evil?" It is reported variously of Socrates or of Plato that each morning he thanked heaven for having been born male and not female, free and not slave, Greek and not barbarian. The implication is that these are disparate species, final and unalterable. But when Plato and Aristotle speak of slavery they refer to slaves as being such "by nature"; this amounts to implicit acknowledgment of the nature/convention dichotomy and justifies the institution of slavery on the only grounds possible if the dichotomy is accepted. In another climate the institution was justified on the ground that slaves were the children of Ham, whom his father Noah had condemned to eternal servitude: "Cursed be Canaan; a servant of servants shall he be to his brethren."

To attribute human institutions to nature is to class them with such inanimate and inalterable phenomena as gravity or the saltness of the sea. In the Old Testament this can be done, for the earth and all it contains are equally the handiwork of God. To deny the validity of one part of God's handiwork is as presumptuous as to deny another. But if human institutions are on a different footing from gravity no godlessness need be involved in questioning their validity. No Greek thought of saying "In the beginning Zeus created heaven and earth." Zeus came into power in a world already existing; and having begun in time he would presumably end in time, and have successors as he had had predecessors. Though poets might represent gods as causing storms or earthquakes to express their displeasure, basically their position vis-à-vis nature was analogous to man's. Realizing the limitations of divine power, therefore, and asserting independence where the divine jurisdiction did not run, would not then imply rebelliousness or carry a burden of sin. If man is not the master of his fate he is and should be the captain of his soul. It is so in Homer and it is so in tragedy.

But it must not be forgotten that it was not so for all Greeks and throughout Greek history. The notion that gods and men occupy disparate spheres and that man is therefore free to manipulate the prescriptions of tradition may have affected life and literature from Homer onwards, but until it was crystallized in the enlightenment of the later fifth century B.C. it was amorphous and dormant. Both before the enlightenment and after it many men, probably the majority, believed not only in a divine providence but in divine surveillance over the affairs of men. One strand of Greek thought, which is represented by the Orphics and then by Plato, among others, and which can therefore claim an important place in the picture of Greek convictions, believed in a dualism of body and soul, taught that the body should be suppressed for the sake of the soul, and held out the hope of a blessed future for souls purified and liberated from their bodies. Hesiod, who may be as ancient as the *Odyssey*, believes in the virtual sovereignty of Zeus (he uses "Zeus" and "the gods" interchangeably) and in his concern for justice. He begins his *Works and Days* with a glorification of Zeus which reads like a Psalm:

For easily he makes strong, and easily he brings the strong man low; easily he humbles the proud and raises the obscure, and easily he straightens the crooked and blasts the proud—Zeus who thunders aloft and has his dwelling most high.

But Hesiod's teaching is in polar contravention of the Biblical "Obey them that have the rule over you," and in contravention too of the Homeric code. In Homer powerful individuals ride roughshod over weaker men; Hesiod is critical of folk-devouring princes bent on their own advantage. Attributes which are complimentary in Homer—proud, strong-spirited, having prowess in arms—take on a pejorative sense in Hesiod; his own epithets of approval are truthful, never-lying, oath-keeping, law-abiding, righteous. His gospel is the gospel of hard work; competition between potter and potter, builder and builder, beggar and beggar, singer and singer, is wholesome and beneficial. It is good for neighbor to compete with neighbor in pursuit of wealth, and it is good to enjoy the respect of your fellow men because your barn is full. But wealth must be earned by strenuous work, not seized. The path which leads to goodness is long and steep, and it is rough at the first; but when a man has reached the top then it is easy, though it was hard before. People who rely on their own strength do not realize how much greater the half is than the whole.

The whole is justice. Might does not make right for men; for fishes and beasts and winged fowl Zeus has ordained that they should devour one another, for right is not in them, but to mankind he gave right, which proves the best. Zeus has thrice ten thousand sprites who roam, clothed in mist, all over the earth and keep watch on judgments and wrongdoing of mortal men; these report misconduct to Justice, who then informs her father Zeus, who ordains punishment.

Often even a whole city suffers for a bad man who sins and devises presumptuous deeds, and the son of Cronos lays great trouble upon the people, famine and plague together, so that the men perish away and their houses become few, through the contriving of Olympian Zeus.

Guilt is communal, for the whole city is made responsible for the transgression of an individual, and it is hereditary: if the malefactor escapes, punishment is visited upon his descendants after him.

If Hesiod be discounted as ancient and provincial with theological and didactic interests, his influence on the main stream of Greek thought is unquestionable. In a later century much of his doctrine is reflected in the widely traveled and sophisticated Solon. Solon was an Athenian merchant and statesman of the sixth century, and his political and social reforms laid the foundation for the Athenian democracy. His utterances may be taken to represent a high and wide intellectual level. Most germane to the present context is his fine prayer to the Muses; because the piece is not generally familiar and because its every clause deserves study it is worth reproducing in its entirety:

O ye fair children of Memory and Olympian Zeus, ye Muses of Pieria, hear me as I pray. Grant, that I may be blessed with prosperity by the gods, and that among all men I may ever enjoy fair fame; that I may be as a sweet savor to my friends and a bitterness in the mouth of my enemies, by the ones respected, by the others feared. Wealth I do indeed desire, but ill-gotten wealth I will not have: punishment therefor surely cometh with time. Wealth which the gods give cometh to a man as an abiding possession, solid from the lowest foundation to the top; but that which is sought with presumptuous disregard of right and wrong, cometh not in the due course of nature. It yieldeth to the persuasion of dishonest practices and followeth against its will; and soon there is joined thereto blind folly which leadeth to destruction. Like fire, it taketh its beginning from small things; but, though insignificant at first, it endeth in ruin. For the works of unprincipled men do not continue long. Zeus watcheth all things to the end. Often, in the spring season, a wind riseth suddenly and disperseth the clouds, and, stirring up the depths of the surging, barren sea, and laying waste the fair works of the husbandman over the surface of the corn-bearing earth, cometh to the lofty habitation of the gods in heaven and bringeth the blue sky once more to view; the sun shineth forth in his beauty over the fertile earth, and clouds are no longer to be seen. Like such a sudden wind is the justice of Zeus. He is not, like mortal men, quick to wrath for each offense; but no man who hath an evil heart ever escapeth his watchful eye, and surely, in the end, his justice is made manifest. One man payeth his penalty early, another late. If the guilty man himself escape and the fate of the gods come not upon him and overtake him not, it cometh surely in aftertime: the innocent pay for his offense—his children or his children's children in later generations.

Thus all we men of mortal mold, good alike and bad, think, by straining every nerve, to win a fair name, each man for himself by his own unaided efforts, until something befall him from without: then straightway cometh pain. Till then like gaping fools we amuse ourselves with empty dreams. He who is worn by cruel disease pondereth ever how one day he will be whole; another, who is a coward, thinketh himself brave; another still counteth himself handsome, though he have no beauty of body; if one be penniless and subject to the toils of poverty, he assureth himself that he will sometime win great riches.

One man seeketh wealth from one source, another from another. This one wandereth in ships over the fishy deep in his eagerness to bring home a profit, the sport of the cruel winds, staking his life ungrudgingly. Another, whose labor is with the curved plow, cleaveth the fertile soil, drudging the year round like a slave. Another learneth the arts of Athena and skillful Hephaestus and gathereth a livelihood by the work of his two hands. Another, trained by the grace of the Olympian Muses, understandeth to the full the sweet art of minstrelsy. Another hath been endowed by the Lord Apollo, who worketh from afar, with the gift of prophecy; and, if the gods attend upon his ways, he discerneth, while it is still far off, the evil which approacheth his fellow. But it is sure that neither bird nor sacrificial victim will avert what Fate ordains. Others are physicians and practice the craft of Paeon, who knoweth many drugs. But no success crowneth their work: often great suffering groweth out of a little pain, and none can bring relief by administering soothing drugs; often, again, one who is overcome by cruel disease may be straightway restored to health merely by the touch of a hand.

Destiny bringeth to mankind both good and evil, and the gifts which come from the immortal gods are not to be refused. Danger, we may be sure, followeth all the works of men, and none knoweth, at its beginning, which way an undertaking will turn. One man, though he is trying to acquit himself well, falleth unaware into great and dire misfortune. Another, who playeth his part ill, is blessed with good luck by the gods and granted release from his folly.

No visible limit is set to wealth among men. Even now those among us who have the largest fortune are striving with redoubled energy. What abundance of riches could satisfy us all? Increase of goods cometh to mortals by the gift of the gods. But out of it appeareth the madness which leadeth to destruction, and when Zeus sendeth this madness as a punishment to men, it lighteth first upon one and then upon another.

(Translated by IVAN LINFORTH*)*

Here too wealth is good, reputation desirable, righteousness essential, punishment inexorable. But guilt is still hereditary: "If the guilty man himself escape . . . the innocent pay for his offense—his children or his children's children in later generations." The notion of hereditary and of communal guilt was by no means limited to the Greeks; it has existed among other peoples, ancient and modern, and was part of popular Hebrew belief also. But both Greeks and Hebrews sensed its injustice and presently revised it. When the Lord purposed to destroy Sodom for its sins (Genesis 18) Abraham could protest, "Wilt thou also destroy the righteous with the wicked?" The prophet Ezekiel objects to the current saying, "The fathers have eaten sour grapes and the children's teeth are set on edge"; the truth is that "the soul that sinneth it shall die." A precisely parallel correction of unenlightened tradition is implicit, as we have seen, in the *Eumenides* of Aeschylus, where the inauguration of trial by jury puts an end to the notion of hereditary guilt and establishes the principle of individual responsibility. Even religious tradition can be amended.

But may not the culprit evade punishment by dying before it can overtake him? The answer to this difficulty, in several theological systems, is a theory of rewards and punishments in a future existence. It is hard to know how early the conception of a future world where the apparent flaws in justice would be rectified obtained currency among Greeks. It is usually associated with the Orphics, but it is present in Pythagoras and possibly in Sappho and it is elaborated in Plato's vision of Er at the end of the *Republic,* which is imitated in similar visions as late as Plutarch. Rewards and punishments in a future existence are firmly outlined by Pindar. Though he was a contemporary of Aeschylus, Pindar's thought belongs to an earlier and stabler world and is untouched by the leaven of the Athenian democracy. Here is Pindar on judgments in the world to come, from the Second Pythian Ode:

But verily, wealth adorned with virtues bringeth the fitting chance of divers boons, prompting the heart of man to a keen and eager quest, wealth which is that star conspicuous, that truest light of man. But if, in very deed, when he hath that wealth, he knoweth of the future, that immediately after death, on earth, it is the lawless spirits that suffer punishment—and the sins committed in this realm of Zeus are judged by One who passeth sentence stern and inevitable; while the good, having the sun shining for evermore, for equal nights and equal days, receive the boon of a life of lightened toil, not vexing the soil with the strength of their hands, no, nor the water of the sea, to gain a scanty livelihood; but, in the presence of the honoured gods, all who are wont to rejoice in keeping their oaths, share a life that knoweth no tears, while the others endure labour that none can look upon—. But, whosoever, while dwelling in either world, have thrice been courageous in keeping their souls pure from all deeds of wrong, pass by the highway of Zeus unto the tower of Cronos, where the ocean-breezes blow around the Islands of the Blest, and flowers of gold are blazing, some on the shore from radiant trees, while others the water fostereth; and with chaplets thereof they entwine their hands, and with crowns, according to the righteous councils of Rhadamanthys, who shareth for evermore the judgment-seat of the mighty Father.

(*Translated by* J. E. SANDYS)

The neatest contrast between the traditionalist outlooks of a Hesiod or a Pindar and the "enlightened" views discussed earlier in the chapter is afforded by their respective theories of the origins and sanctions of human society. At first, according to the *Works and Days,* there was a golden race of men who lived like gods, remote from toil and grief and blessed by easy abundance of all good things. Then came a much inferior race of silver, whom Zeus suppressed for their wrongdoing and replaced with an age of bronze, which in turn destroyed itself by its contentiousness. Then came the race of heroes, who were destroyed in the wars at Thebes and Troy. The fifth race, which now occupies the earth, is a race of iron; men never rest from labor and sorrow by day and from perishing by night. This race too is doomed to destruction as wickedness multiplies among men. Eventually Aidos and Nemesis (shame which restrains men from wrong; righteous indignation) will forsake mankind to join the gods; bitter sorrows will be left for mortal men, and there will be no help against evil. The direction of human history is steadily from bad to worse.

Hesiod's sequence is exactly reversed in the rationalist view implicit in the teaching of the Sophists and carried to an extreme position by the Epicureans. Our fullest account of the rationalist view is in Lucretius's poem *On the Nature of the Universe,* which is as late as the first century B.C. and in Latin, but there can be no doubt that it presents older Epicurean doctrines. Men started out not in a state of prelapsarian bliss but as uncivilized primitives. They formed societies for better protection against enemies animal and human, created laws to protect the physically weak and make society viable, specialized functions for ampler commodity, and introduced other improvements as expediency suggested to meet emerging challenges. Something of the same process is suggested in the sketch of the development of society in Plato's *Republic,* but there the improvements themselves are signs of corruption: ampler diet causes illness, which requires doctors, and ampler wealth instigates envy on the part of neighboring peoples and necessitates a standing army. But in Lucretius the direction is not from happiness to misery but the other way around, and the responsible agents are not the gods but men themselves. No contrast could better illustrate the implications of man the measure for attitudes towards traditional authority. The very history of the race is made to show that such tradition is without binding force.

At several points in his *Works and Days,* Hesiod shows affinities to Near Eastern thought which seem too close to be accidental. Many of his prudential apothegms are like the wisdom of the Egyptian Amenhotep or of the Biblical Book of Proverbs which is related to it; the most striking parallel of all is his story of the fall of man through the importunate curiosity of a woman. Pandora is the Greek Eve; it was she who removed the lid from the jar and allowed the calamities that plague mankind to escape into the world. The only thing that was caught by the rim and shut back into the jar was Hope. What was Hope doing among Bad Things? Is she not a Good Thing, to be bracketed with Faith and Charity? Perhaps she is not for the pragmatic Greeks, even so devout a one as Hesiod. Perhaps she only confuses practical reality. When Prometheus lists his benevolent gifts which could make the hard lot of man tolerable he mentions the art of healing and drugs and then hope, apparently a desperate anodyne when the resources of the pharmacopeia are exhausted. Hope that the schoolhouse will burn down is neither a reasonable nor a salutary solution for a boy afraid of an examination; he had better use his time to prepare or to inquire about admission to a trade school. Even so pious a pagan as Hesiod cannot be expected to have that faith which is the substance of things hoped for, the evidence of things not seen.

Sentimentality of any kind seems suspect to the Greeks because its outlines are blurred and its results unpredictable. Preference for the pragmatic and the definable is not limited to rationalists but is a common trait characteristic of the general Greek outlook. That is why even people essentially conservative could feel free to manipulate tradition and why such an essentially unworldly system as Stoicism was based, as we shall see, on a rationalist logic. The distinction is not between believer and nonbeliever but between Greek and non-Greek.

CHAPTER 4
ARISTOCRATIC DEMOCRACY

The aspects of Greekhood which we have dealt with so far, and those yet to be dealt with in three chapters following, are all components or reflections of the characteristic Greek style. It was adherence to their code of style which enabled the Greeks to survive the revolution of the Hellenistic Age and perpetuate Greek values in non-Greek lands. But a special code implies an elite. Concern for its transmission is motivated by solicitude for cherished tradition, but it might also be interpreted as a jealous effort to perpetuate prerogatives of rank. All aristocracies have had their own codes, less attractive than Hellenism, it may be, and sometimes mitigated by the principle of noblesse oblige, and have sought to perpetuate their exclusiveness. Why did not the exclusiveness of the elite produce a caste system in Greece, as it did in India for example, with only a fortunate minority as bearers and beneficiaries of the code? How did a whole people come to share the outlooks we expect of an exclusive aristocracy?

The philosophic rationale which made egalitarianism possible has been described above. Since men are equal in nature, and rank is the product of convention, society may be fluid rather than static; since the social structure had been evolved by men and not imposed by divine authority, revolution involves no impiety, and since man is the measure of all things, assertion of self and pursuit of excellence is a desirable goal open to talent. These notions explain how exclusiveness might be broken, an aristocracy dislodged or supplanted, and its outlooks come to be shared by the generality. We must now look at the processes by which the potential came to be realized, and then to be curbed.

Our earliest records suggest that the Greek code too was limited to an elite; the paradigms which served to propagate Greekhood for centuries after the heroic age were all aristocratic in nature. The *Iliad* is a thoroughly aristocratic poem. Its personages are described as god-born or godlike, which is tantamount to a patent of nobility. Fighting is by single combat, in the knightly mode; there must have been lesser warriors, but these are seen only in dim masses. The only toilers we see are those figured on the shield of Achilles; the only workaday pursuits, like farming or herding, occur in the humbler poet's own similes. Glory is the driving force and the object of existence. Birth, wealth, and prowess in arms and in speech confirm a man's title and give him the right to whatever he can win. The only man who questions the code is Thersites. Though Thersites too is "godlike," he is represented as repulsive in appearance and behavior, and there is universal applause when Odysseus, who represents the interests of the group, belabors him. Sarpedon's exhortation to Glaucus (*Iliad* 12.310 ff.) might have been uttered by any lord in a society of knightly warriors:

Why, Glaucus, are we so specially honored in seats and meats and full cups, why do all men look upon us as gods? Why are we allotted wide demesnes on the shores of the Xanthus, rich in vineyards and grain-bearing tilth? Therefore it becomes us to take our place in the forefront of the Lycians and to wage flaming battle, so that some man of the well-armed Lycians will say, Not ingloriously do our princes hold sway over Lycia, eat fat sheep and drink choice sweet wine; their prowess is great when they fight at the forefront of the Lycians. If, friend, avoiding this battle we could live ageless and deathless, I myself would not fight among the foremost nor would I urge you to glorious battle; but a myriad fates of death impend which mortal man can neither escape nor evade. Let us therefore march forward; we shall give glory to someone or someone to us.

It speaks for the enduring vitality of the Homeric code, and also for the character of Alexander the Great, that Alexander carried the *Iliad* about with him in a jeweled casket and slept with it under his pillow.

The *Odyssey* is probably later than the *Iliad* in date and is much later in spirit. Here the hero gains glory by long and profitable voyaging, by intellectual resourcefulness rather than prowess in arms; Odysseus too is "godlike," but his kind of distinction depends more on individual achievement than on blood lines, and so glory comes nearer to being a career open to talent. The *Works and Days* of Hesiod (who, unlike Homer, was a mainland Greek) marks not merely a deviation from the Homeric code but a revolution against it. Here the common man emerges, and shows his restiveness under aristocratic misrule. Folk-devouring princes are bad; good men must work hard and unceasingly and be prudent and thrifty. A full barn is a fine thing to have, but not the least of its advantages is that it will win a man admiration and respect. Glory is still a very desirable thing, but now it is a goal to which all free men might aspire. In social structure as in government and religion Hesiod's world was very different from Homer's; the one tradition that persisted, and continued to persist, was the drive towards individual distinction.

The war elegies of Callinus of Ephesus and Tyrtaeus of Sparta, both of the seventh century, look more Homeric in their admiration for warlike prowess, but in fact deviate significantly from the Homeric ideal. The soldier is exhorted to fight bravely because courage brings practical advantages as well as glory and cowardice practical disadvantages as well as disgrace. The soldier is a citizen before he is a hero. He fights not in single combat but in a line with his fellow citizens; his reward is not abstract glory but the esteem of his countrymen and security for himself and his family. Archilochus, who was a professional soldier as well as a poet, shows how far the externals of the heroic code could be flouted while its essentials were preserved. He not only threw his shield away but wrote a poem to advertise the wisdom of his act.

The simple agricultural economy reflected in Hesiod was complicated by the introduction of coined money, which enabled the rich to accumulate capital for lending and business ventures and increased the disparity between rich and poor. In Attica farms were mortgaged at ruinous rates, and when the impoverished borrowers could not pay, not only was their land taken but they themselves were sold into slavery. In many cities professed protectors of the commons, themselves usually of the noble class, usurped authority and became "tyrants." The term received its opprobrious connotations only later, during the full-blown democracy; actually many of the tyrants proved enlightened and beneficent rulers, concerned to establish a viable dynasty. By suppressing the high-handedness of the nobles to the advantage of the commons they did in fact promote the rise of democracy.

In Athens the advent of tyranny was postponed by the liberal legislation of Solon, who was archon in 594, which laid the basis for the Athenian democracy. Solon enacted a moratorium on mortgages, forbade enslavement for debt, threw the assembly open to all freemen, gave the court of the Areopagus new powers, and created a new Council of Four Hundred. Despite this amelioration or perhaps because of it (now radicals could say that as a tool of the rich Solon made the minimum concessions to prevent revolution) tension between classes continued, and after a generation Pisistratus succeeded in making himself tyrant. Pisistratus and his sons Hippias and Hipparchus were effective rulers and promoted the cultural flowering of Athens; among other things they instituted the annual dramatic competitions at the theater of Dionysus and established the practice of reciting all of Homer at the annual Panathenaic festival. The tyrants not only broke the exclusiveness of the aristocrats, then, but spread aristocratic outlooks and interests among the whole people. Hippias was exiled in 510 and the constitution was further liberalized in the direction of democracy by Clisthenes, who was a member of the Alcmeonid clan, the principal rivals to the Pisistratids.

It was the democracy which had to face the great invasion of the Persians, in 490 and 480, which was encouraged by the exiled Hippias, and only a democracy, according to Herodotus, could have defeated the overwhelming Persian force. Neither Herodotus in his history of the Persian War nor Aeschylus in his play about it shows the Persians as other than brave and loyal and cultivated men. The decisive difference between the adversaries is that the Greeks were free and the Persians were not. It was their freedom which enabled the Greeks to conquer the Persians, and the ample reward of their victory was the continuation of this freedom. When a Persian grandee offers Spartan envoys wealth and preferment in return for submission, they tell him (Herodotus 7.135): "Hydarnes, you are a one-sided counselor. You have experience of half the matter but the other half is beyond your knowledge. A slave's life you understand, but never having tasted liberty, you cannot tell whether it be sweet or no. Had you known what freedom is, you would have bidden us fight for it, not with the spear only but with the battle-ax." "It is plain from many instances everywhere," Herodotus says in his own person (5.78), "that freedom is an excellent thing; since even the Athenians, who while they continued under the rule of the tyrants were not a whit more valiant than any of their neighbors, no sooner shook off the yoke than they became decidedly the first of all."

For our present concerns, what is most remarkable about

---

the Athenian resistance is that it was undertaken against the advice of Delphi, which counseled submission. Though Delphi had no means of exacting obedience from the Greek states, it was the nearest thing the Greeks had to a central authority and its prestige was traditionally very high, not only in its proper sphere of religion but in political guidance also. When the Greeks nevertheless chose to fight for liberty in spite of Delphi they demonstrated that their loyalty to a peculiar style outweighed obedience to the spokesmen of recognized religious and political tradition.

The states that joined the resistance against the invaders did so not for the sake of an abstraction called Greece but each for its own safety. Repeatedly the Spartans, who had the strongest land force, sought to withdraw their contingents and post them at the Isthmus of Corinth to protect their home country alone; they were dissuaded from doing so only by the Athenians' threat to withdraw their navy and so permit the Persians to turn the Spartan defense by landing at their rear. Some Greek states not only refused to cooperate with the resisters but actively "Medized," that is, aided the invaders. A congress of patriotic states did pronounce sanctions against them, but they were never read out of the community of Greeks. What may seem more shocking, not all the leaders of the resistance continued steadfast in their patriotism after the victory; here too there was a notable defection to the Persian side. Eventually Themistocles himself, who was the moving spirit of the resistance and himself directly responsible for the victory at Salamis, went to serve the Persian king though the Persians were still a lively threat to Greece.

Nothing shows the Athenians' jealous care to maintain democratic equality as dramatically as the institution of ostracism. By the process of ostracism (which lapsed at the beginning of the Persian War) Athens sometimes ejected its best citizens who had done no wrong at all but merely because an outstanding individual who might seem to become indispensable was not a wholesome thing for a democracy. If as many as six thousand of his fellow citizens wrote a man's name down on their voting sherds (*ostraca*), he was banished from the state. How ill-advised the practice could be is shown by the story of Aristides called the Just. At a voting for ostracism a man unable to write asked Aristides himself to write "Aristides" on his sherd for him. When Aristides asked what complaint he had against the man, the answer was that he did not know Aristides at all but was tired of hearing him called "the Just."

The Persian War not only preserved the Athenian democracy but multiplied the citizen body which enjoyed its benefits and so secured it against reactionary movements. Greek soldiers furnished their own weapons, so that the branch in which a man served was determined by property qualifications. The result was that the army became an upper-class institution. Owning and maintaining a horse was a mark of wealth in Attica, and accordingly the wealthiest classes served in the cavalry. In the Athenian democracy its numbers were small and it was seldom used. The next financial class, who were the mainstay of the citizen body as of the army, served as hoplites. These were men who possessed landed property and were capable of providing full armor for hand-to-hand combat. The poorer citizens, who had no property and no military equipment, served in the so-called light-armed troops. Eventually they were provided with light shields and throwing spears and were employed as a regular arm in conjunction with the hoplites, but in the early fifth century they were mustered only in emergencies, for offensive or defensive action in sudden border conflicts.

But the exigencies of the Persian War required that Athens greatly enlarge its navy. The decisive action was by sea, and after the victory the expectation that Persia might strike a third time naturally placed Athens at the head of the defensive Delian League. As head of the Delian League, and then as mistress of the empire into which the

League was insensibly transformed, Athens necessarily became primarily a naval power. It was because of Athens' naval might that Pericles could regard the territory of Attica as expendable, fifty years later, and thus venture upon the Peloponnesian War. The Spartans marched in and devastated the countryside, as they were expected to do, but instead of marching out to resist them with the hoplite force the Athenians stayed within their walls and relied upon the navy to convoy subsistence from abroad.

The new importance of the navy as the prime element in the city's defense caused a shift in the political balance. The personnel of the navy were not independent landholders but landless men who were paid for their service; indeed a collateral advantage, if not motivation, for maintaining the navy is that it provided work and pay for an urban proletariat. It had been calculated that some 12,000 men were in active naval service for some eight months of each year, and they and their dependents were enough to eclipse the political importance of the hoplite class. More important, outlooks characteristic of an upper class could now be shared by the generality. "We alone regard a man who takes no interest in public affairs," Thucydides makes Pericles say in his Funeral Oration, "not as a harmless, but as a useless character."

The same Funeral Oration contains Pericles' celebrated glorification of the Athenian democracy. A patriotic harangue need not be accepted as an objective description, but it does at least show what the audience would like to believe about themselves. Here then is how the Athenians thought they differed from other people:

Our form of government does not enter into rivalry with the institutions of others. We do not copy our neighbors, but are an example to them. It is true that we are called a democracy, for the administration is in the hands of the many and not of the few. But while the law secures equal justice to all alike in their private disputes, the claim of excellence is also recognized; and when a citizen is in any way distinguished, he is preferred to the public service, not as a matter of privilege, but as the reward of merit. Neither is poverty a bar, but a man may benefit his country whatever be the obscurity of his condition. There is no exclusiveness in our public life, and in our private intercourse we are not suspicious of one another, nor angry with our neighbor if he does what he likes; we do not put on sour looks at him which, though harmless, are not pleasant. While we are thus unconstrained in our private intercourse, a spirit of reverence pervades our public acts; we are prevented from doing wrong by respect for the authorities and for the laws, having an especial regard to those which are ordained for the protection of the injured as well as to those unwritten laws which bring upon the transgressor of them the reprobation of the general sentiment.

And we have not forgotten to provide for our weary spirits many relaxations from toil; we have regular games and sacrifices throughout the year; our homes are beautiful and elegant; and the delight which we daily feel in all these things helps to banish melancholy. Because of the greatness of our city the fruits of the whole earth flow in upon us; so that we enjoy the goods of other countries as freely as of our own.

Then, again, our military training is in many respects superior to that of our adversaries. . . . Whereas they from early youth are always undergoing laborious exercises which are to make them brave, we live at ease, and yet are equally ready to face the perils which they face.

We are lovers of the beautiful, yet simple in our tastes, and we cultivate the mind without loss of manliness. Wealth we employ, not for talk and ostentation, but when there is a real use for it.

(*Translated by* BENJAMIN JOWETT)

This picture of the Athenian temperament seems to be corroborated in the Corinthians' appeal to the Spartans before overt hostilities began:

You have never considered what manner of men are these Athenians with whom you will have to fight, and how utterly unlike yourselves. They are revolutionary, equally quick in the conception and in the execution of every new plan; while you are conservative—careful only to keep what you have, originating nothing, and not acting even when action is most urgent. They are bold beyond their strength; they run risks which prudence would condemn; and in the midst of misfortune they are full of hope. Whereas it is your nature, though strong, to act feebly; when your plans are most prudent, to distrust them; and when calamities come upon you, to think that you will never be delivered from them. They are impetuous, and you are dilatory; they are always abroad, and you are always at home. For they hope to gain something by leaving their homes; but you are afraid that any new enterprise may imperil what you have already. When conquerors, they pursue their victory to the utmost; when defeated, they fall back the least. Their bodies they devote to their country as though they belonged to other men; their true self is their mind, which is most truly their own when employed in her service. When they do not carry out an intention which they have formed, they seem to themselves to have sustained a personal bereavement; when an enterprise succeeds, they have gained a mere instalment of what is to come; but if they fail, they at once conceive new hopes and so fill up the void. With them alone to hope is to have, for they lose not a moment in the execution of an idea. This is the lifelong task, full of danger and toil, which they are always imposing upon themselves. None enjoy their good things less, because they are always seeking for more. To do their duty is their only holiday, and they deem the quiet of inaction to be as disagreeable as the most tiresome business. If a man should say of them, in a word, that they were born neither to have peace themselves nor to allow peace to other men, he would simply speak the truth.

(Translated by BENJAMIN JOWETT)

It is to be expected that the head of a state at war should invoke "respect for the laws . . . and the unwritten laws," but at about the same date as the Funeral Oration Sophocles makes his Antigone reject a lawful edict out of loyalty to what she believes is the unwritten law. The *Antigone* is one of several plays (the *Philoctetes* is another) in which Sophocles discusses the rights of individual judgment as against the claims of the state—which shows that the problem was a living one to his audience. Here is the gist of the argument. When Haemon approaches his father Creon to appeal on Antigone's behalf, Creon refuses: "Whomsoever the city may appoint, that man must be obeyed, in little things and great, in just things and unjust. . . . Disobedience is the worst of evils. This it is that ruins cities. . . . Therefore we must support the cause of order." Haemon appeals to reason and to popular opinion: "Father, the gods implant reason in men, the highest of all things that we call our own. . . . The dread of your frown forbids the citizen to speak such words as would offend your ear; but I can hear these murmurs in the dark. . . . 'No woman,' they say, 'ever merited her doom less, none ever was to die so shamefully for deeds so glorious.' . . . If any man thinks that he alone is wise, that in speech or in mind he has no peer, such a soul when laid open is always found empty." Sophocles, it must be noted, was not a revolutionary but a notably pious man with high respect for authority and orderliness. But even a pious and dutiful Athenian could take an independent attitude against constituted authority.

Even after Athens lost the Peloponnesian War and was impoverished, the qualities which Thucydides praised and the relative freedom of individual judgment which Sophocles reflected continued recognizable. The next great crisis was the rise of Macedonian power under Philip, which eventually brought Athenian sovereignty to an end. Among the first to recognize the danger was Demosthenes, who was an admirer of Pericles and his ideals, and he devoted his magnificent eloquence to preserve them. But the older Isocrates, who foresaw a greater peril to Greekhood from the East, urged a union of the disparate Greek states, of which he invited Philip to become leader, with a view to an eventual Greek crusade in the east. For a partisan of the Athenian democracy it is natural to applaud Demosthenes, as most such partisans have done, and to deprecate Isocrates' program as an invitation to tyranny and a dilution of pure Hellenism. But in the light of subsequent history Demosthenes may in fact have been romantically attached to a past that was proving anachronistic, and it was Isocrates who had a truer vision of the future. But the prelude of the spread of Hellenism was Philip's defeat of the combined Athenian and Theban forces at Chaeronea in 338 B.C., and Isocrates did not live to see Philip's son Alexander carry his program to realization. In the words of Milton's sonnet,

> As that dishonest victory
> At Chaeronea, fatal to liberty,
> Killed with report that old man eloquent.

Athens could no longer maintain an independent foreign policy but it did maintain the democratic style of the *polis*, and, as we shall presently see, planted democratic *poleis* in the new lands Alexander conquered.

CHAPTER 5

PHILOSOPHIC
AUTARKY

Philosophic inquiry is the most characteristically Greek of all Greek preoccupations because it is the most obviously humanist. To take an independent stand outside the phenomena of the world and self and to examine both without inherited prejudice is truly to make man the measure of all things. Children and old men and men asleep cannot be called happy, says Aristotle in the *Ethics,* because human happiness demands the exercise of what is peculiarly human in man's nature. What this is Aristotle declares in the opening sentence of his *Metaphysics:* "Man by nature desires to know." This is not exhortation but definition. A fish who gives up swimming is no longer a fish; a man who does not activate the desire to know is either protracting infancy or anticipating senility or vegetating.

What is common to all the Greek philosophers, from the pre-Socratics of the sixth and fifth centuries B.C. down to Roman times, is the unremitting effort to find some principle of homogeneity and stability in the apparent confusion of the material world, some rational order in the phenomenon of man. Systematic thought is based on a combination of perception and inference. What our senses perceive is heterogeneous, localized, dated; but by a process of abstraction we can infer the universal principles at the root of the data presented by our senses. The search for the permanent and universal is as applicable to ethics as it is to physics.

Are we swayed by sensation or reason? Do we live in a world of appearance or reality? Do we mistake opinion for knowledge? Why and how, and can you maintain your position if I argue its opposite?

We smile at the early pre-Socratics of the East, the so-called Ionian physicists, who conceived of all matter as composed of Air, Earth, Water, and Fire. But it requires a strong and agile intellect to envisage order and uniformity where appearances are so varied and so confused. These men differ in degree but not in kind from the modern chemist with his table of atomic weights, or from Socrates seeking a different kind of universal reality behind appearances. The pre-Socratics of the West, in Sicily and Italy, leaned towards mystical teaching, but that is because philosophers were expected to make all knowledge their province. Empedocles could compose one work entitled *Purifications,* and without incongruity another entitled *On Nature.* Pythagoras's wider fame rests upon his spiritual doctrine, but he was also a great pioneer in mathematics. A more important and more universal insight of all these Greeks is that science must be systematic and verifiable and pure. A saying attributed to Pythagoras runs: *Skhama kai bama, ou skhama kai diobolon,* "New diagram another advance; not, new diagram another dollar."

Of Socrates it was said that he brought philosophy down to the world of men, and he did indeed shift the direction given to philosophy by the pre-Socratic physicists. But his modes of investigation were not essentially different from theirs, and it was not out of obscurantism that he neglected natural science. His object, as he is made to say in Plato's *Apology,* was to sting men into the realization that an unexamined life is not worth living. For self-examination the most efficient and economical procedure is to draw a distinction between opinion and knowledge, between appearance and reality. And what the examination is expected to yield is clarification, not a set of prescriptions.

In the early dialogue called *Euthyphro* Socrates' interlocutor is a man who prides himself on piety. What is piety? Socrates needs to know, for he has been indicted for impiety. Euthyphro answers by offering illustrations of pious conduct. But what is the principle which makes a kind of conduct pious? What is the universal which gives character to the particular? Doing what the gods approve, Euthyphro suggests. Good enough; but this brings up another small question: Is a thing pious because the gods approve of it, or do the gods approve of it because it is pious? At this point Euthyphro remembers another engagement. Piety has not been defined (nor are similar abstractions in other early dialogues), but fuzziness has been cleared away, and we are nudged into looking more narrowly at ourselves and our place in the world instead of accepting traditional opinions without examination.

The practice of the tragic poets, who were serious investigators, concerned not primarily with producing *belles lettres* but with probing man's psyche and his reactions to other men, was essentially similar. Their regular procedure was to take some bare and in itself meaningless headline out of mythology, say "Medea murdered her children," and then to make the headline credible and useful by analyzing the various pressures which might impel a woman to commit such a deed or deter her from it, the reactions of those affected by the deed, and its implications for the rest of us. Thucydides' history is in effect an objective study of the morphology and psychology of war. In comedy and pastoral we approach the actual techniques of experimental science. In the *Birds* of Aristophanes or in Longus' *Daphnis and Chloe* a prepared field is deliberately rigged, in heaven or in a secluded valley, chosen subjects are placed in it, they are exposed to a series of stimuli, and their reactions are observed and recorded. In the one case we have a demonstration of the sociology of a city, in the other a study of how young people fall in love. If we protest that the city and the young people are only figments, the Greek literary critic, Aristotle for example, would retort that imaginative creation is truer than literal chronicle.

For Plato, who is the principal channel of Socratic thought, the reality of which the ephemeral world we know is only a dim reflection has an independent and eternal existence, and it is this reality to which examination of life must lead. But another devoted follower of Socrates, Antisthenes, directed his examination to the conventions of this world and found them based on opinion rather than knowledge. His better-known disciple, Diogenes of Sinope (400–325 B.C.), made his whole career a continuous warfare against convention and glorification of "life according to nature." Because he did in public what conventional people do in private he was called *Cyon* ("dog") for his shamelessness, and his followers were called Cynics ("the doggish ones"). His was the first school to engage in street-corner preaching, and his evangelists apparently peppered their discourses with homely stories of the master, all of which illustrate his resistance to convention. When he saw a real dog lap water from a puddle he threw his cup away. When Alexander asked what favor he could do him, he said, "Step out of my light." When asked to what city he belonged, he answered that he was a citizen of the world (*cosmopolites*), implying that he rejected the vaunted superiority of particular Greek city-states as being without basis in nature. He carried a lamp by day to find an honest man. He declared that his object was to spoil the coinage— the same Greek word means "currency" and "convention."

Diogenes' disciple was the more sensitive and more charitable Crates, who renounced wealth and position to take up his master's scrip and staff and ragged cloak. "I am a citizen of the lands of Obscurity and Poverty, impregnable to Fortune, a fellow citizen of Diogenes," he is reported to have said (Diogenes Laertius 6.93). It was from Crates, apparently, that Zeno, the founder of Stoicism, caught his vision of a polity coextensive with the *oikoumene* or inhabited world. "Zeno's earliest work," writes W. W. Tarn, "his

Republic, exhibited a resplendent hope which has never quite left men since; he dreamed of a world which should no longer be separate states, but one great city under one divine law, where all were citizens and members one of another, bound together not by human laws but by their own willing consent, or (as he phrased it) by Love." Zeus, providence, the world, are really one; all men are portions of the divine, and therefore all are equal. In universal nature there is no distinction between Greek and barbarian, slave or freeman. Each man, whether statesman or laborer, performs the function assigned him, with no pride of place and no diminution of dignity. Certain of Zeno's predecessors, as we have seen, had advocated an independent approach to gradations of class and to other traditional institutions, but none had proposed a program so revolutionary as to envision the abolition of all existing sovereignties.

In all respects the ethical ideal of the early Stoa was perfectionist; what is not wholly right is still wrong, for what is not perfectly straight is crooked. External circumstances —position, wealth, even family and health—are "things indifferent"; man must preserve his *apathy* or freedom from passions and cultivate his inner self. A cobbler who has attained spiritual perfection is a king, a king who has not is a cipher. In course of time Stoics abated their stark perfectionism and were content with gradualism and a program of amelioration, but even five centuries after the founder it could still animate a pure spirit like Marcus Aurelius, who was the most powerful figure in the world and still regarded himself not as the master of the Roman Empire but its servant. Traditional values of human dignity and decency continued under Stoicism, then, with only minor shifts of emphasis; its revolutionary political program may have continued to affect men's dreams, but the Stoics themselves ceased to hope for its imminent realization. What is important from our present viewpoint is the expectation that humanity could transcend revolutionary change in environment.

Stoicism was one response to a central problem of the Hellenistic Age (of which we shall speak more fully in the sequel)—that of redressing the imbalance between diminished man and his overwhelmingly enlarged world. Stoicism's strategy was to enhance the importance of man; its pendant, to make the world less important than it seems, was the way of Epicureanism. What makes the world seem important, and what constricts the individual, is the powerful structure of political organization and the weight of traditional beliefs. In order to liberate the individual from these constrictions the Epicureans put forward the most systematic of all programs for differentiation between nature and convention and became the most thoroughgoing of all advocates for freedom from the bonds of official tradition. At all points the program of Epicureanism seems to be a calculated refutation of Platonism. For the Epicureans the world is thoroughly and exclusively materialistic. It and all things in it are composed of fortuitous concatenations of atoms moving about in absolute emptiness, and nothing else. Phenomena thought to be willed by the gods, like thunder and earthquake, can be explained by the motion of atoms and need posit no divine intervention. Sight, hearing, dreams, which were taken to prove the independent activity of the soul, are only extensions of the physical sense of touch. The soul is composed of finer atoms, but at a man's death all his atoms disperse, and since there is no survival of personality there can be no question of rewards and punishments after death. There are indeed gods, but they too are composed of atoms: they are wholly indifferent to man, unaffected by his prayers or his virtues or vices, and pass their time in a kind of divine picnic. There is no design, no providence, no sanction external to man, and no spiritual goal for his aspiration. Man is therefore wholly independent, and his own sole guide is the principle of pleasure, which is defined as avoidance of pain. His goal is ataraxy, or unruffledness. Morality, then, is not adherence to a code prescribed by tradition, unless adherence affords pleasure; it is in effect a prudent balance between pleasures and the pains they may entail. If a man indulges himself to such excess that the hangover outweighs the pleasure his error was in arithmetic, not in violating a code. The orgies which were charged to the Epicureans consisted less in eating and drinking and being merry than in geometry, for the pleasures of geometry entail the least amount of pain. It is easy to see why a system which set up no authoritative code of behavior and which denied any divine concern with the affairs of men should be anathema to Jews and Romans and Christians who believed that a divine providence governed the world and that they were its favored objects.

Epicureanism endured for centuries and had many adherents down to the end of pagan antiquity, but they had no appetite for agitation, for that would impinge upon ataraxy. In their daily lives, therefore, they were not noticeably different from other men. They were good neighbors, loyal friends, conscientious family men, and diligent in business. They might, like Cicero's Epicurean friend Atticus, avoid political entanglements when these might endanger their ataraxy, but Epicurus himself advised his followers to participate in religious festivals. To adherents of a religion which is centered upon doctrine and claims exclusive truth this seems logically inconsistent: should not a man who denies all obligations to the gods eschew all religious observances? The point to remember is that Greek religion was less a matter of doctrine than a matter of cult practices, which need entail no theological beliefs. That is the logic of Christmas trees in homes of infidels today. That is why pagans were genuinely puzzled when Christians, whose deviant beliefs they could acknowledge, refused to participate in communal festivities with religious associations. Cult is mainly a matter of style, the forms of outward conduct which set a society apart from outsiders. If the enlightened Greeks rejected tradition as a valid guide to ideas they gave it the highest importance as a valid guide to style.

All Epicurean teaching seems motivated by opposition to one or another aspect of Platonism. The Academy itself continued in being, but became increasingly "academic" in the modern pejorative sense. Gradually its doctrine was transformed, partly under the influence of the more vital competing schools. Early in the Hellenistic Age, in the so-called New Academy, Platonism grew skeptical; no positive position could be taken on any subject, for only proba-bility, not absolute knowledge, is attainable. A lawyer like Cicero, for whom Stoicism was too perfectionist and Epi-cureanism too permissive, professed himself an Academic. Later still Platonism was influenced by a recrudescence of Pythagoreanism, and the way was thus paved for the mysti-cism of the Neoplatonists. In its later stages even more pro-nouncedly than in its earlier, Platonism was centered on the individual man. The non-Aristotelian writings in the corpus of Aristotle show that the Peripatetic school re-tained its character as a research institution, devoted to scholarship rather than philosophic speculation. But schol-arship too is a means of asserting individuality.

In that it practiced and encouraged independent specu-lation on the world and man, all Greek philosophy tended to enhance the importance of the individual. In the Hel-lenistic Age, when "first philosophy" fell into decline and the individual was in greater danger of being overwhelmed by the suddenly enlarged world, teachers of philosophy made it their special object to emphasize the importance of individual man. There is a functional relationship between their teachings, especially those of the Stoics, and the highly individualized portraiture of the age. When the classics of philosophy, like the classics of literature, came to be virtually canonized, the law of contradiction, which respected no *ipse dixit,* fell into abeyance, not to be fully resuscitated until the age of the humanists. Philosophizing was reduced to exegesis of the old masters, and was no longer independent and uninhibited inquiry. But the old classics continued their function of safeguarding individuality; the writings of the Hellenistic teachers in particular were popularized and rendered into Latin, and so served to perpetuate the sense of the importance of the individual, which is an essential of humanism.

But there was another element of the humanistic tradition to which the entire philosophic enterprise had contributed but which was of special concern to the Hellenistic Age—the idea of the unity of mankind. This too persisted through the ages and received new vigor in the age of the humanists. For the crisis of our time it has acquired special urgency; we turn therefore to a brief consideration of the fortunes of the ecumenical ideal.

CHAPTER 6
THE ECUMENICAL IDEAL

Where mankind is conceived of as the product of a special act of creation and the object of a continuing providence, superiority and inferiority of races, or as we have learned to say, advanced and retarded peoples, are what they are by divine election and their status is therefore immutable. But where man is a product of his own evolution from the primitive, the basic equality of the species is premised, and degrees of advancement or retardation are due to circumstances of environment or training. There is no impassable barrier to prevent the retarded, in a more favorable environment and with superior training, from becoming the equals of the advanced and sharing their advantages. The valid differentiation among men is between the intelligent and the stupid, and both kinds are found among Greeks and non-Greeks alike. The Greeks generally took the scientific rather than theologic view of the development of man. They were convinced of their own superiority to lesser breeds, at some periods more blatantly than at others, but they recognized the potentialities of other peoples also, and eventually conceived of the whole known world as an *oikoumene* in which all should be members one of another.

Homer conceived of mankind as uniform, and the pre-Socratics offered a scientific rationale for the conception. In Homer the armor and religious outlooks and manners of

---

the Trojans are no different from those of the Greeks, and their heroes are as heroic and as chivalrous. The foreign contingents in the Trojan host speak different languages, as do the Cretans also, and Egyptians and Phoenicians have peculiar characteristics, but they are not despised. The Cyclopes and the Laestrygonians are subhuman giants outside the world of men. There is even a premonition of the biological basis of human equality which later philosophers would make explicit: all men have speech, all eat bread, all are wretched, and all must die. So Odysseus can take all mankind into his somber generalization: "Of all that breathe and move upon the earth, earth breeds no creature frailer than man."

No one could be less parochial than Herodotus. He gives a sympathetic account of the various peoples in the ancient world, noting the character and customs of each and despising none, however much they differ from the Greek norm. There must have been a widespread interest in strange peoples and politics, for Hecataeus, whom Herodotus occasionally cites to correct some fault, had written a detailed account of foreign places. Herodotus's catholicity is well illustrated by an experiment he reports of Darius (3.38):

Darius, after he had got the kingdom, called into his presence certain Greeks who were at hand and asked what he should pay them to eat the bodies of their fathers when they died. To which they answered that there was no sum that would tempt them to do such a thing. He then sent for certain Indians, of the race called Callatians, men who eat their fathers, and asked them, while the Greeks stood by and knew by the help of an interpreter all that was said, what he should give them to burn the bodies of their fathers at their decease. The Indians exclaimed aloud and bade him forbear such language. Such is men's custom; and Pindar was right, in my judgment, when he said, "Custom (*nomos*) is king over all."

(*Translated by* GEORGE RAWLINSON)

Custom is king, but the very existence of customs shows that they are artificial manifestations of an essentially identical humanity.

Herodotus's account of the Persian Wars (which is his proper subject) communicates no sense of the victory of an innately superior people over an inferior, like the wars of Israelites against Canaanites or of Romans against Gauls. The vanquished are as civilized and as brave as the victors. After the exhilaration of the victory literature and art do show the Easterners as unreliable and effeminate. The foreigners whom the Greeks encountered, usually as slaves, were probably not the best representatives of their people. But the conception of unitary humanity persisted. The famous ode glorifying man in the *Antigone* of Herodotus's friend Sophocles begins: "Wonders are many, and none is more wonderful than man"—not "than Greek man."

The theoretical uniformity of mankind was provided with a scientific rationale by the pre-Socratics. Anaximander held that primitive men originated as fishlike creatures formed out of warm slime before earth and water were separated. If their development thereafter proceeded at varying paces, their essential nature must still be the same. The Hippocratics insisted that identity of biological functions proved mankind a single species. Apparent variations in outward appearances are due to differing environments and are merely superficial. Heraclitus made *logos,* speech and rationality, the common gauge of humanity. The proper distinction between men is not according to race but according to intelligence. The conception of equality is based on biological function, and distinctions are determined by intelligence rather than race. The Sophist Antiphon used Hippocratic reasoning to deny the validity of the class structure and the Sophist Protagoras said that knowledge could be taught. The history of Thucydides, which is concerned with universal laws of the behavior of man in war, is posited upon an assumption that human nature is a universal, and the same may be said of the ethical philosophers, beginning with Socrates.

Isocrates advertised Greek superiority but attributed it to intelligence and declared that a non-Greek with Greek education was in effect Greek. The pupils of Isocrates who wrote history did not confine themselves to Greece but wrote universal histories. Isocrates had urged the Greeks to unite for a large-scale invasion of Asia; the invasion was carried out, a generation after his death, by Alexander the Great. And it was Alexander, consciously or otherwise, who gave the ideal of the union of mankind a measure of realization. But when, near the end of his life, he caused Macedonians and Persians to intermarry and adopt similar dress the notion of union must have taken shape in his mind. Here is the account of a solemn festival of union at Opis as told by the sober Arrian (7.11):

After this Alexander offered sacrifice to the gods to whom it was his custom to sacrifice, and gave a public banquet, over which he himself presided, with the Macedonians sitting around him, and next to them the Persians, after whom came the men of the other nations, preferred in honor for their personal rank or for some meritorious action. The king and his guests drew wine from the same bowl and poured out the same libations, both the Grecian prophets and the Magians commencing the ceremony. He prayed for other blessings, and especially that harmony and community of rule might exist between the Macedonians and the Persians. The common account is that those who took part in this banquet were 9,000 in number, that all of them poured out one libation, and after it sang a song of thanksgiving.

(*Translated by* E. J. CHINNOCK)

Whether or not it was Alexander's design to amalgamate all people of the earth, we can believe of Aristotle's pupil that he distinguished people according to intelligence rather than race. Here is a report of Eratosthenes, an Alexandrian scholar of the second century B.C., given by the geographer Strabo (1.4.9):

Towards the end of his treatise—after withholding praise from those who divide the whole multitude of mankind into two groups, namely, Greeks and barbarians, and also from those who advised Alexander to treat the Greeks as friends and the barbarians as enemies—Eratosthenes goes on to say that it would be better to make such divisions according to good qualities and bad qualities; for not only are many of the Greeks bad, but many of the barbarians are refined—Indians and Arians, for example, and, further, Romans and Carthaginians, who carry on their governments so admirably. And this, he says, is the reason why Alexander, disregarding his advisers, welcomed as many as he could of the men of fair repute and did them favors.

(Translated by H. L. JONES)

But even if the picture of Alexander as the unifier of mankind is apocryphal, the construction and dissemination of the picture show that the ideal was familiar to the hearts and minds of men, who could look back on it with longing and hope. Here is the picture drawn some three centuries after Alexander's death in the youthfully florid essay of Plutarch called *On the Fortune of Alexander* (330 CE):

Alexander did not overrun Asia like a robber nor was he minded to tear and rend it, as if it were booty and plunder bestowed by unexpected good fortune, after the manner in which Hannibal later descended upon Italy, or as earlier the Treres descended upon Ionia and the Scythians upon Media. But Alexander desired to render all upon earth subject to one law of reason and one form of government and to reveal all men as one people, and to this purpose he made himself conform. But if the deity that sent down Alexander's soul into this world of ours had not recalled him quickly, one law would govern all mankind, and they all would look toward one rule of justice as though toward a common source of light. But as it is, that part of the world which has not looked upon Alexander has remained without sunlight.

(Translated by F. C. BABBITT)

If Alexander himself was not the great visionary that the yearnings of humanity in later antiquity and in modern times have made him to be, there can be no doubt that Zeno and the early Stoa did in fact teach the brotherhood of man and desiderate the realization of their ideal even at the cost of the subversion of all existing institutions. The same essay of Plutarch makes Alexander the strong secular arm for Zeno's teaching (329) :

Moreover, the much-admired *Republic* of Zeno, the founder of the Stoic sect, may be summed up in this one main principle: that all the inhabitants of this world of ours should not live differentiated by their respective rules of justice into separate cities and communities, but that we should consider all men to be of one community and one polity, and that we should have a common life and an order common to us all, even as a herd that feeds together and shares the pasturage of a common field. This Zeno wrote, giving shape to a dream or, as it were, shadowy picture of a well-ordered and philosophic commonwealth; but it was Alexander who gave effect to the idea.

(Translated by F. C. BABBITT)

Cynic–Stoic popularizers were an important factor in promoting a sense of the unity of mankind. But what the Stoics made a positive doctrine, the rival school of the Epicureans, who were an equally influential force in the Hellenistic world, taught out of negativism. Their absolute materialism put conventional distinctions of race and class wholly out of the question. They were in fact a universal solvent. As Cicero scornfully put it, "Those who guide their lives by pleasure can be happy wherever pleasure is available—as Teucer remarked, 'My country is wherever things go well with me.' "

Epicureanism was frowned upon in Rome, because Rome could not tolerate its indifference to all authority. But Rome itself did more than Alexander had done to realize the ecumenical ideal. Its emperors sometimes made themselves masters instead of Stoic ministers for administering the affairs of the brotherhood of man. But, in Rutilius's line, Rome did make a city of the world. And there was even an emperor who conceived of the world as a single city; here is the Emperor Marcus Aurelius (4.4):

If to understand and to be reasonable be common to all men, then is that reason, for which we are termed reasonable, common unto all. If reason is general, then is that reason also which prescribeth what is to be done and what not, common unto all. If that, then law. If law, then we are fellow-citizens. If so, then the world is as it were a city. For which other commonwealth is it that all men can be said to be members of?

(*Translated by* MERIC CASAUBON)

When the writers of the humanist age resumed the ancient dialogue the unity of mankind was an important element of it. Like Thucydides, Machiavelli analyzes the political motivations of all men, not Italians alone. The enlightened views of Erasmus and of Thomas More are not addressed to Dutchmen or Englishmen but to all who could read Latin, and those of Rabelais and Montaigne to all Europeans. And presently the humanistic tradition which these men carry forward becomes truly ecumenical; when Darwin and Marx and Freud take it up the scope of its relevance has become world-wide. The ecumenical ideal is not the least of the strands in the humanist skein; in the world which we must now envisage it is one of the most important.

CHAPTER 7

THE CODE OF STYLE

The complex of outlooks and modes of conduct which we have glanced at in the preceding chapters found its fullest expression in Athens but was understood and to varying degrees shared by all Greeks; it was loyalty to this complex rather than to a central political authority that gave the scattered and politically disparate Greeks such consciousness of unity as they had and reinforced their sense of being different from other peoples.

For the Hebrews and for the Romans their national histories, enshrined in an actual or virtual scripture, constituted a kind of charter which welded the people together into a proud unity with a common past, common ideals, and common aspirations. Each believed that it was a divinely chosen elect, that its career had been directed by a special providence, and that this providence would continue to lead it to its manifest destiny. The scriptures prescribed forms of government and rigorous codes of conduct, but they also exacted a consuming loyalty. Modern authoritarian states have sought to devise some such mystique of their own in order to ensure solidarity. The Greeks had no such sacred history and no national charter to define their identity. What did define it, create a sense of kinship among them, and set them apart from other peoples was their common concept of humanism.

In their great age the Greeks had no central authority, political or religious, to prescribe any kind of uniformity, and except for *ad hoc* alliances no political confederations to promote common action. The only really effective *ad hoc* alliance was that against the non-Greek invaders from Persia, and even here, though orators invoked the common ideals of Hellenism, the independent city-states entered the alliance only because their individual safety was immediately and obviously endangered. Those which thought they could come to terms with the Persians did not participate in the common defense of Greece. The Peloponnesian War, which was longer and harder than the Persian, was fought between Greeks, the city-states of Athens and Sparta and their allies. The relation of the disparate states to the abstraction we call Greece was therefore analogous to the relationship of the nationalities of Europe to the abstraction we call Europe, not that of the states of our union to the United States of America. To a lesser degree than the states of our union but to a greater than the nations of Europe the city-states of Greece had linguistic, religious, and other cultural affinities with one another, and like the nations of Europe they were more likely to vie with one another than with "barbarians." Nor did "Hellas" have so precise a geographical connotation as does "Europe," for all communities of Greeks, in Asia Minor, southern Europe, and northern Africa as well as in the Greek mainland and the islands of the Mediterranean, were recognized as sharers of Hellenism.

The Greek conviction of superiority had its rationale. Greek is to non-Greek, Isocrates said, as man is to animal. Man possesses *logos,* which means "word," "discourse," "rationality," and animals do not. Greeks are superior to non-Greeks because they possess numerous and subtle and refined *logoi.* They can not only discourse more profoundly and about many more things, but their discourse is more élegant. Isocrates goes so far as to say that the preeminence of Athens, not only in literature and art but in diplomacy and war, is due to the inimitable superiority of its *logoi.* Indeed "Greek" is defined not by race but by education; a non-Greek who possesses the liberal education of the Greeks (*paideia*) becomes a Greek, and by corollary a racial Greek who does not is not truly a Greek. Here is Isocrates' central statement on the subject (*Panegyricus* 47–50):

Practical philosophy, moreover, which helped to discover and establish all these institutions, which at once educated us for action and softened our mutual intercourse, which distinguished calamities due to ignorance from those which spring from necessity, and taught us to avoid the former and nobly to endure the latter, was introduced by Athens; she also paid honour to eloquence, which all men desire, and begrudge to those who are skilled in it: for she was aware that this is the only distinguishing characteristic which we of all creatures possess, and that by this we have won our position of superiority to all the rest of them; she saw that in other spheres of action men's fortunes are so capricious that often in them the wise fail and the foolish succeed, and that the proper and skilful use of language is beyond the reach of men of poor capacity, but is the function of a soul of sound wisdom, and that those who are considered clever or stupid differ from each other mainly in this respect; she saw, besides, that men who have received a liberal education from the very first are not to be known by courage, or wealth, or such-like advantages, but are most clearly recognized by their speech, and that this is the surest token which is manifested of the education of each one of us, and that those who make good use of language are not only influential in their own states, but also held in honour among other people. So far has Athens left the rest of mankind behind in thought and expression that her pupils have become the teachers of the world, and she has made the name of Hellas distinctive no longer of race but of intellect, and the title of Hellene a badge of education rather than of common descent.

(*Translated by* J. H. FREESE)

If the measure of any civilization, then, is the interval from the animal, manifested in articulate speech and rationality, the measure of Greek civilization is the refinement of thought and conduct and taste which grow out of these capacities. In other words, civilization consists in the habit of transcending animal reflexes, and this the Greeks believed they did more artfully and more fully than other people. The appropriate designation for the habit of civilization artfully achieved and practiced effortlessly is *style,* not necessarily a particular style, for style is subject to refinement and development, but style itself regarded as a force. If the tradition of style should perish civilization would have to begin again from the start; if Greek style should be interrupted Greekhood would disappear. That is why the Greeks took the utmost pains to imbue oncoming generations with the values of Greek style.

The repository of Greek style was a library of ancient books, much the same as those we call classics today, and because all Greeks were made familiar with their contents these books were the principal means of transmitting Greek style from generation to generation regardless of where and under what government Greeks lived. Style had been so transmitted from the earliest days of epic recitations; by Isocrates' day and through his influence the program of education in style had become explicit. Isocrates trusted books (as we shall see Plato did not) to communicate the outlooks appropriate to Greekhood; the repository was now laid open to all men, and each could draw from it according to his capacity. When the center of Greek education shifted to Alexandria the ancient books were not only collected into "canons" but the collection was virtually canonized in the sense that the collection we call the Bible was canonized; it is significant that all litterateurs to the end of antiquity (and following their example those beyond) cited the books of the canonical collection very frequently but very rarely modern or recent works.

The central item in the canon and the mainstay of education was always Homer. It is not true to say, as was once the fashion, that Homer was the bible of the Greeks, for *Iliad* and *Odyssey* are secular books with no claim to supernatural authority; but these were the books every Greek knew, as New England Puritans knew the Old Testament, and their values were therefore accepted with as little question as we accept the facts of the multiplication tables. There are echoes of Homer in virtually every subsequent Greek author, frequently in the form of direct quotations or adaptation. Though he was reputed to be expert on all practical matters from cookery to horse breeding (and could be made to seem so by deft interpretation), unlike Scripture Homer is seldom invoked as an authority for orthodox doctrine. His function is rather as an exemplar for correct bearing, sometimes in deportment and sometimes in literary expression. It was not the legendary Trojan War as a segment of history that made Homer an instructive text, for there were very much larger and more recent wars that affected men's lives more directly better suited for historical study; nor was it the tragedy of Achilles, for there were later princes, Alexander the Great at their head, whose lives were fit subjects for tragedy. Homer continued the mainstay of Greek education because he is the repository of Greek style.

Homer's hero, and hence the hero of Greekhood, is Achilles. For all his starkness Achilles is a simple and vivid exemplification of calculated deviation from the animal. In the first place he had been given a choice between a long but commonplace life and a short but glorious one. In choosing the short life (and in his subsequent choices) for the sake of glory Achilles in effect transcended the animal instinct for survival; as parallel transcending of reflexes in another spiritual climate we might think of turning the other cheek or walking the second mile. But Achilles is very far from being a Christian or a typically European hero. He is fairly obsessed with self, and recognizes no sanction except that of his own ego. The code he lives by is his own independent achievements, and these range from mastery over enemies and rivals to mastery over self. Both his ruthlessness and his high courtesy are manifestations of his special style. Because his passions are so powerful mastery over them is not easy. When they drive him to the point of attacking Agamemnon in open meeting, in the first book, he is recalled to his proper style by a glance from Athena and restores his sword to its scabbard. The intensest passion of all is to disgrace the body of Hector, who had killed his friend Patroclus, and even this passion he masters, at the end of the book, and restores the body to Hector's father Priam for honorable burial. This is a high point in the *Iliad,* and, one is tempted to say, in all Western literature. His private style Achilles exhibits, among other situations, in his reception of Agamemnon's ambassadors in *Iliad* 9. Achilles beguiles his leisure with music, entertains his guests graciously, bases his rejection of their invitation on a mature philosophic discourse.

Achilles himself is aware of his style and knows when he abdicates it. In the final battle with Hector, Hector had attempted to parley: If I kill you I promise to return your body to your people for proper burial, and do you agree to do the same for me. Achilles replies that no pact is now possible, any more than it would be between animals— which is as much as to say, I am no longer Achilles but an animal, for I have laid my style aside. Before the combat Hector was naturally afraid, for he knew that Achilles was the mightier warrior. But he was heartened when he looked behind him and saw what he took to be his brother carrying a spare weapon. But when, having missed his first blow, he turned to obtain the fresh weapon, the "brother," who was in fact a phantom sent by Athena, had vanished. What appears to be a piece of divine treachery is actually a grace, bestowing on Hector a style he himself might be incapable of. His death had been decreed by fate, and no Olympian could prevent it; without the phantom he would have turned tail and received Achilles' spear in his back. Now he receives it in his chest, which is where a gentleman should have it. The difference between these antagonists is exemplified in their mothers. Thetis is ineffably graceful and detached and aristocratic; Hecuba a care-worn Mediterranean mother, consumed with anxiety for her child.

The monumental dignity and the high sense of their own worth natural to the Homeric heroes make the reader feel they are twice the stature of ordinary flesh and blood, but though even an Achilles is not ashamed to weep, the narrative is never distorted by sentimentality and never exaggerated to the point of incredibility. What made Homer a usable text so many centuries after it was written is its directness and simplicity and truth. When a mighty hero is confronted by a dangerous enemy and has spent spear and sword he lifts a boulder to hurl that two—but only two—men of the present generation could scarcely lift. In Apollonius of Rhodes the ratio will be an incredible six to one and in Vergil an impossible twelve to one. When Helen appears to the Trojan elders on the wall they acknowledge in their grasshopper voices that such beauty is worth fighting for, but their sanity is not dissolved into sentimentality; "even so," they say, "let her go upon their ships, and not stay to vex us and our children." Glaucus and Diomedes forgo their duel, when they find their fathers had been friends, and decide on a courteous exchange of weapons instead, Glaucus's gold for Diomedes' bronze. If we find such cavalier indifference to monetary value hard to believe, so did Homer also; we know that it is fact and not sentimental embroidery when he remarks that Zeus bereft Glaucus of his wits in that he accepted the value of nine oxen for the value of a hundred. Hector boasts of more than he achieves and takes credit (for the slaying of Patroclus) which he has not fairly earned, but his dignity is undiminished even when he is chased three times round the walls of Troy, and the sympathy he evokes is grave rather than sentimental.

The aristocratic ideal of Homer's heroes persisted into less heroic ages. Hesiod's outspoken opposition shows that the ideal was still to be reckoned with in his day. In Theognis of Megara (sixth century B.C.) blood and breed are paramount, and the effect of wealth in obliterating distinctions of race is deplored. Why, when such care is taken in choosing livestock for breeding, Theognis asks, are aristocratic lines permitted to degenerate for the sake of profitable marriages? "The good" in Theognis means the aristocrats, and "the bad" the lower classes. In Athens at least, largely through the legislation of Solon, the result of the amalgam was that the commoners came to share the outlooks which had been the preserve of the nobles: all became "the good." In the century following, Pindar, who was an immeasurably greater poet than Theognis, continues Theognis's bias towards aristocracy. His grandiose epinician odes were commissioned by the princely houses which still held sway in the peripheries of the Greek world, and the atmosphere of aristocratic brilliance in which he moves is at the opposite pole from Hesiod's. The gorgeous aura of purple and gold through which he sees his noble figures makes Homer almost commonplace, and yet the highest praise he can bestow on his patrons is to suggest, by the lineage he assigns them and the legends of the heroic age which he weaves into his poems, that they are comparable to the heroes of old.

The aristocratic houses which he served were already an anachronism in Pindar's time and would soon be abolished, but the heroic ideal had not lost its effectiveness. It is obviously operative in Aeschylus, Pindar's Athenian contemporary, who was devoted to the democracy. It permeates not only the *Oresteia* and the *Seven against Thebes,* whose plots derive from the ancient heroic cycles, but also and most significantly the *Persians,* which deals with the war in which Aeschylus himself had fought. The Greek personages in the *Persians* are contemporary Athenian democrats and yet they are somehow endowed with the same remote grandeur as the figures from ancient legend in the other plays. The stature of these figures is undiminished in Sophocles, and they continue to wear their heroic habiliments even in Euripides, though he sometimes parodies them.

Tragedy was another essential of later Greek education, and tragedy exhibits heroic dignity and truth like Homer's. The plays do indeed offer strong and simple archetypes of the fundamental crises of humanity and of the precariousness of human existence, but that was not their sole function in the schools. Nor was it to exhibit specimens of virtue and vice and their consequences for moral edification, nor as a discharge for turbulent passions which might otherwise prove troublesome. The actions are indeed often scabrous and mean; the *Agamemnon* itself can be reduced to a lurid story of a sultry love triangle. But neither Aeschylus nor his readers so reduce it. Behavior which a less civilized art would present as harrowing or maudlin is regarded with a monumental kind of heroic detachment. The plots of Sophocles are as strenuously passionate as any in the human repertory, but the poet's art lends them a civilized serenity unaffected by time and the vagaries of taste. That is why Sophocles was styled the most Homeric of the tragic poets, and that is why he is a useful adjunct to Homer for communicating the ideals of Greekhood.

In Sophocles' day the climate of the heroic age was of course an anachronism, as it had doubtless been when the Homeric poems first took their present form. Not long after Homer himself, a rustic moralist like Hesiod could take exception to the high-handed injustice of the Homeric heroes and advocate a more practical bourgeois code. In the later fifth century, Euripides, as has been observed above, questioned the morality and usefulness of the heroic legends; a play like *Iphigenia at Aulis,* for example, shows Menelaus and Agamemnon as pompous, ambitious, and ineffectual politicians, Achilles as a braggart soldier, Clytemnestra as a middle-class matron attracted by an advantageous marriage for her daughter. The true heroine, whose selflessness makes the rest of the cast look tarnished and vulgar, is the simple and pitiable Iphigenia. Euripides' language and versification correspond to his lowered key; as compared with the elaborate poetic techniques of Aeschylus and Sophocles his plays (except for the choral interludes) are a close approach to ordinary prose. *Iphigenia at Aulis* is not only the last of Euripides' plays; it marks the end of Greek tragedy of the heroic type. The ancient plots and personages were too exhausted to serve a living theater. The invented plots and dramatis personae of New Comedy, which was the natural successor of Euripidean drama, were frankly contemporary types. But if drama forsook the heroic ideal, the ideal retained effectiveness in other genres and to some degree even in drama itself.

Of the changes in climate Sophocles, who was Euripides' elder but outlived him, was surely aware. His adherence to tradition was not conscious archaizing to produce museum pieces but a programmatic effort to preserve the values of heroism and of high art. To a man who could say that not to be born is best and next best to die betimes, life is utterly tragic. Only by the high bearing of the heroic code could dignity be wrested from it and only through the refraction of high poetry could it be clothed with beauty. It can be plausibly argued that Sophocles' *Electra* is a purposeful correction of Euripides', and his *Trachinian Women* of Euripides' *Medea*. In Sophocles Electra is not a slatternly and psychotic nymphomaniac but a lady of stature whose dignity is enhanced by suffering. Dejaneira, like Medea, is impelled by a domestic crisis to use a poisoned garment, but she does so unwittingly. She is not a passionate barbarian bent on murderous revenge but a dignified Greek matron seeking to preserve a respectable home. The heroic climate may have grown remote but it was not stale. On the contrary, the task of preserving it was now more urgent.

The object of the classical poets was not merely to produce *belles lettres* but to communicate salutary doctrine; and when Isocrates invented his artistic prose, early in the fourth century, and insisted that artistic prose was a proper vehicle for important content, poetry of the heroic kind, both epic and tragic, fell into decline. In the third century it experienced a shadowy revival in Alexandria, but there the predominant interest was literary preciosity. The implications of literary style for our subject we shall examine in the chapter following; here we must see how Alexandrian and later works may have contributed to maintaining the ancient ideals. In Alexandria we hear of a "pleiad" of seven tragic poets, whose work was never performed and apparently not much read, but their subjects were drawn from the traditional repertory and presumably reflected the ancient ideals. The writings of the pleiad have perished, but we do have some 265 lines of a tragedy on the Biblical Exodus, called *Exagoge,* by one Ezekielos, who is said to have written other plays on Biblical themes also. What is of interest here is that non-Greek saga highly revered by its own heirs is assimilated to Greek norms. Whether the object of men like Ezekielos (he was not unique) was to advertise Biblical tradition to pagans or to make it more acceptable to Jews who had received Greek education, the point to notice is that the heroic Greek ideal is the lens through which non-Greek tradition is seen and the criterion by which it is judged. Even more remarkable in this respect, if it is not a mere literary exercise, is the extant *Christus Patiens,* ascribed to Gregory of Nazianzus (fourth century) but probably of much later date. Though no liberties are taken with the Christian Passion, the story is told largely in Euripidean tags stitched together and hence takes on an archaic Greek flavor. Through various changes in outlooks and beliefs the classics continued to be esteemed as the acknowledged repository of Greek style.

The latest reverberation of classical tragedy in antiquity are the plays of Seneca, written (but probably not performed) in the first century A.D. These are direct adaptations of particular Greek tragedies of the fifth century. They lack, indeed, the profound spiritual probings of their originals and tend rather to rhetorical display and to sensationalism verging on the ghoulish. But even if their characters sometimes stretch the measure of their Greek patterns and the violence of their passions to the point of monstrosity, they do propagate, as they premise, a degree of familiarity with the classical norms and the classical ideals. What is more important, they communicated these ideals to Europe; through Seneca the Greeks inspired and informed the tragedy of the humanist age, of the Elizabethans in England and of the dramatists of the golden age in Spain. The content of drama changed, from the Greeks, to Seneca, to the humanists; what persisted through all the vicissitudes was a quality of style.

The establishment of the great library at Alexandria gave new incentives and new depths to the study of the classics, and fostered new creations also. It was mandatory, as we shall see, for new compositions to follow the forms of the old, and it was therefore natural that they should, to some degree, reflect the outlooks of the old also. For propagating the heroic outlook, epic, as we should expect, proved more effective than tragedy, not only in Alexandria but in Rome and its progeny also. From Alexandria we have the *Argonautica* of Apollonius of Rhodes; the subject of this epic is the quest of the Golden Fleece by Jason and his comrades, who antedated the Trojan War. Apollonius's main object may have been to parade his own antiquarian erudition and his technical virtuosity, but surely concomitantly to propagate familiarity with heroic tradition. Any creative writer dealing with a remote age is liable to commit anachronisms; we can see, if Apollonius could not, that his psychological description of Medea's love is too subtle and too romantic for the heroic age. Sometimes his Alexandrian sophistication introduces a jarring note that seems intentionally comic. Hera and Athena decide that Jason's only hope is for Medea to fall in love with him and call on Aphrodite to enlist the help of her son Eros. The visit of the grand Olympian ladies to the flustered and unkempt blacksmith's wife makes a delightful genre scene. Aphrodite remarks on the difficulty of getting children to obey, finds Eros busy beating Ganymede in a game of dice, tempts him with a pretty ball, and receives his winnings to hold for him—after he has carefully counted them. No joke need be intended in such incongruities, for Apollonius was doubtless unaware that he was confounding Olympian and contemporary Alexandrian manners. But even if he is aware of the incongruity, as Fielding obviously is in Molly Seagrim's epic fight in the churchyard, it is not the epic mode which is ridiculed; rather it is the pattern by which deviations from it are made ridiculous. Indeed, Apollonius's sophistication makes his respect for the ancient style of gods and heroes the more remarkable. Beliefs, like customs, might change and the style itself adapt to the new environment; but it was still a high style and carefully kept removed from the ordinary.

Vergil clearly thought Apollonius's intentions were serious, for he imitated him in his utterly sober *Aeneid;* in particular, the loves of Aeneas and Dido in *Aeneid* 4 follow the loves of Jason and Medea in *Argonautica* 3. Unlike the *Argonautica* (or any Greek work) the *Aeneid* is an institutional poem, intended to glorify the beginnings of Rome, its founder, and its mission. It is therefore natural for Aeneas to be given heroic stature. But the armature for his grandiose image, an image bequeathed to all subsequent heroes of European epic, was suggested by Greek convictions of proper heroic style.

CHAPTER 8

THE
LITERARY
VEHICLE

Style in bearing and outlook is one and perhaps the more important aspect of the Homeric legacy; a more tangible aspect, and one easier to trace, is the literary style which gave the outlooks their power to survive. Like his subject matter, the stately roll of Homer's hexameters, the ornamental epithets and formal similes, the repeated formulaic phrases, the spaciousness of the movement and its purposeful retardations, all derive from a long tradition of oral composition, but here they are legislated into a canon of form of which the salient quality is a monumental dignity. The essential spiritual values may be adapted to the requirements of a later age so that they are not immediately recognized; the Homeric form is copied directly, though it may be refined, and is calculated to be recognized at once for what it is. All ancient epic, Greek or Latin, followed Homeric literary techniques, and all subsequent European epic, whatever the subject, consciously emulated Vergil's emulation of Homer.

From Homer the Greeks, and their posterity, learned that if a man has something significant to communicate he dare not blurt it out but must clothe it in a dignified style and one appropriate to its theme. That is why the Greek classics are classic. When an art attains its appropriate form, Aristotle said, that form is retained. Doric temples, for example, are by no means identical but all follow the same formula. The number of flutings on a column is the same, their contours are similar, the proportion of ends to sides is the same, the arrangement of metopes and triglyphs on the architrave is the same. There is sufficient scope for individuality and for adjustment to terrain in the application of the details of the formula. In the arts as in literature allegiance to traditions of form produced the works we call classic, and the spaciousness and monumentality of classic form imposes itself upon content also.

As Homer fixed the form appropriate for epic so his successors in other genres adapted and fixed their forms also. For more personal instruction on politics or morality, the elegiac couplet is used, as by Solon or Theognis; for more individualistic reflections, the iambic, as by Archilochus or Hipponax; for the large choral lyrics, usually the grandiose triadic structure, as by a series of choral composers, of whom the most esteemed and best preserved is Pindar. What could be more highly stylized than tragedy? People do not ordinarily converse in identical metrical lines of artful language, and their conversations are not normally interrupted by a group of fifteen elders or maidens who dance and sing to comment on what has been said. This is the farthest possible remove from film with sound track to record actual encounters. Tragedy made no pretense of being a transcript from life; it was produced and received as an artistic distillation through the mind of the poet. Decor and costume were as far and as purposefully removed from the familiar as was language; that is why lack of literal verisimilitude in plot or timing, until the relative realism of New Comedy, is not disturbing. So exigent are the canons of form that a reader leafing through a collection of all the playwrights cannot know, from superficial inspection, which play belongs to which author. Not only do all have similar alternation of "spoken" episodes and lyric interludes, but the basic plots and the dramatis personae and the locales recur—just as columns and pediments do in Doric temples. The similarity of form enhances differences in outlook rather than otherwise; Euripides' divergences from his predecessors in social and religious outlooks are not obliterated by the external similarity but rather become more salient.

It might be expected that tragedy should follow tradition faithfully because it was essentially a ritual, might enjoy a reading public as well as a somber audience in the theater, and might even be revived at a later date. But comedy dealt with current affairs, and though it too originated in ritual, it was presented in a carnival mood and in a carnival atmosphere; it is striking evidence of the force of traditional form, therefore, that a genre so flamboyant and so ephemeral possessed a structural pattern as rigorous as that of tragedy and observed it so scrupulously. It happens that Aristophanes, the only comic poet whose works have survived, was a staunch conservative, hostile to the Sophists and the upsurge of the democracy, but here his political and social views are irrelevant. Rival comedians of more liberal temper observed the same traditional forms.

Poetry of the somber kind ceases during the fourth century, not because men had grown indifferent to refinement of form but because they had discovered, through Isocrates, that prose could be made artistic enough to serve as a vehicle for serious substance. When Gorgias of Leontini brought his ornately curled prose style to Athens in 428, the city is said to have gone mad with enthusiasm. Isocrates reduced the excesses of Gorgias; even so his own style with its avoidance of hiatus and its homoioteleuta is as carefully wrought as poetry. Isocrates is called an orator, though he never delivered his speeches; but discourses have to be addressed to someone, and since the essay had not been invented his took the form of orations. Later the problem was solved by epistles, addressed to an individual, indeed, like those of St. Paul or Seneca, but intended for larger audiences. The dialogues of Plato fall into a different category; they are in form what was called mimes or recitation of fictive conversations, a form which the Sicilians Sophron and Epicharmus pioneered and which was again cultivated in the Alexandrian age. It is not until that age that we get what might fairly be called *belles lettres,* art for the sake of art, not for serious communication.

The literature of Athens was truly a folk literature, not in the sense of being inartistic and unsophisticated, but in the sense that it spoke for and to a whole people. The great library at Alexandria, which succeeded Athens as the capital of the literary world, was, as an Alexandrian poet called it, a chicken coop of the Muses. The scholars and writers who worked there were not ministers of a democracy but protégés of the Ptolemies. Though the Ptolemies professed to be legitimate heirs of the Pharaohs and oppressed and exploited the fellahin as their predecessors had done, they were careful to keep administration, army, and commerce in the hands of Greeks or thoroughly Hellenized non-Greeks. There was therefore a practical as well as a sentimental reason (the Ptolemies themselves were of course Macedonians) for ensuring the perpetuation of a class bred to the Greek style, and the means for setting Greeks apart from non-Greeks was the cultivation of Greek literature.

The work of Ptolemy's protégés was both scholarly and creative. The scholarly work was of the kind bestowed on the classics ever since: purifying and editing texts and supplying them with commentaries, lexica, and grammars. New productions might and should emulate the classics but never supplant them. Most of the Alexandrian poets we know were connected with the library, and they are often called scholar-poets, that is to say, scholars first and poets only incidentally. It may well be that poet-scholars is a truer designation. Here were men who were primarily poets, bent on reviving a characteristically Greek art which had long been intermitted, but so exigent were the requirements of correct style that they must first become expert in the traditions of Greek poesy before they could venture to carry them forward. Tradition was the impelling force for scholarship, not the other way around.

The *Mimes* of Herondas are instructive. These came to light in a well-preserved papyrus discovered before the turn of our century. The discovery was sensational, not only because it restored an author who had scarcely been known by name, but because compared to the authentic classics the mimes seemed so vulgar. They show a brothel-keeper justifying his calling in court, a woman gossiping in a shoe shop, a matron angry with an unfaithful gigolo, and other scenes similarly unheroic. The first English translation of Herondas bears the title "A Realist of the Aegean," and one critic declared that Herondas was the first Greek who wrote for people who move their lips when they read. But closer examination reveals that for his meter Herondas chooses the scazon or "limping iamb" which Hipponax had established as appropriate for vulgar poetry some seven centuries earlier, and that he uses words from Hipponax of whose meaning he is no longer certain. So exigent are the requirements of a traditional style that even a vulgar poet addressing a vulgar audience feels obliged to observe them. It is this attention to tradition, indeed, that makes Herondas respectable literature. Actually his material is enlightening and edifying; mime writers were quite properly called "biologists" or "students of life." What might be merely titillating is given philosophical objectivity.

Adherence to correct traditional style, or what was believed to be correct traditional style, did not then exclude innovations in outlook and manner. The herdsmen in Theocritus's *Idylls* (or the literary gentlemen masquerading as herdsmen) are of a class too humble to figure in the classics, and especially in heroic hexameter, and yet Theocritus uses the hexameter, even, most anomalously, for songs. Here as elsewhere it is not traditional style that is the innovation; it is the groundwork against which innovation becomes more striking and more acceptable and the tradition itself more universal.

The major epic of the Alexandrian age is the *Argonautica* of Apollonius of Rhodes, which tells of the quest of the

Golden Fleece (which preceded the Trojan War in time) and of the loves of Jason and Medea which made the quest a success. There can be no question that Apollonius intended to create a heroic atmosphere; the characters are familiar personages of the heroic age, and the hexameters, epithets, similes, and divine interventions are all patterned after Homer's. Only upon reflection do we realize that the bourgeois touches alluded to above introduce a new note, and that a feckless Jason might be a surrogate for the heroic Achilles, with prowess in the field of love substituted for prowess in the field of battle. We could then surmise that the description of the embroidered couch cover on which Jason was at his best takes the place of the designs on the shield of Achilles. These things are not unconscious anachronisms; they too illustrate the phenomenon of innovation against the background of tradition, but the background remains vital.

In the fourth century A.D. Quintus of Smyrna worked the legends of what happened at Troy after the burial of Hector (where the *Iliad* ends) into a fourteen-book epic called *Posthomerica*. Quintus uses Homeric language and techniques correctly and, with no intention to disguise himself or his date, obviously tries to reproduce the authentic Homeric atmosphere. In the sentimentality of such scenes as the death of Penthesilea or the self-immolation of Oenone any reader can discern that the *Posthomerica* must be centuries removed from Homer. But even when the content is changed, the vessel of style can carry its own value. The ideal of the heroic age continues valid, and even for us is the gauge by which deviations can be assessed.

If Quintus intended heroics and lapsed into sentimentality, it was the other way with Musaeus, the fifth-century A.D. author of *Hero and Leander*. Musaeus's story is banal and incredible, like those of the Greek romances, but instead of prose he uses heroic hexameters to give the story specious stature, and instead of the usual happy ending his hero and heroine die pitiful deaths, to make the story a tragedy. If the ideal could not always be reached it re-mained a living force. That Musaeus was right in thinking that traditional form might make even trivial matter viable is proven by Marlowe and Chapman, Schiller and Grill-parzer, who esteemed *Hero and Leander* sufficiently to adapt it in new literary treatments.

The danger of excessive devotion to style is eventual in-difference to content. This point was reached in the second century A.D. in the movement known as the Second Soph-istic, which emphasized a return to classical style in prose and made style alone the criterion of literary merit. Its doctrinaire adherents went so far as to regard any writer who concerned himself with substance as a renegade to their cause. But the movement had a rationale, and not all its works are contemptible. Of the numerous writers of the age the wittiest and most modern is Lucian of Samo-sata. Lucian has been the inspiration of all the "classic" satirists of Europe, and in clever translation he can still sound like a bright and cynical contemporary. Yet despite the modernity of his outlook the prose Lucian writes, in vocabulary and grammar and rhythm, is not that of his own day but that of the fifth and fourth centuries B.C. It is pre-cisely as if a modern insisted on using Elizabethan lan-guage, with *hath* and *doth, thou* and *ye*. A modern who did so we should regard as eccentric—unless he were at prayer. Lucian too, it may be, uses archaism with a kind of reli-gious motivation. When taste in literature and the arts and religion had become vulgarized and their practitioners mercenary, the only feasible prophylactic seemed to be classic style, which might itself preserve the values of sound culture. Essentially Lucian's classicism is romantic, for his picture of the rationality and clarity of the past was ideal-ized, as it was likely to be for a man brought up in Syria. Idealization of the classical age was indeed the first lesson of Hellenism to the cultural provinces of Greece, in the West as in the East.

To educated Romans, all of whom studied Greek, Greek

literature meant the classics, and no Greek work could be acceptable to a Roman audience unless it were couched in classical Greek. Even works whose promulgation was motivated by religious evangelism would be given proper style in order to assure them a hearing. A case in point is Philostratus's *Life of Apollonius of Tyana,* which is an aretalogy, or sacred biography of a revered teacher. Apollonius taught and was reported to have performed miracles in the first century; following the lead of the Church historian Eusebius, he has been dismissed as a charlatan put forward by paganism to discredit the uniqueness of Christ, but there can be little doubt that he was an earnest teacher seriously concerned for the spiritual welfare of his fellow men. Septimius Severus's empress Julia Domna, who was a religious enthusiast, evidently thought so, for she commissioned Philostratus, an eminent litterateur, to write his *Life.* In his proem Philostratus states that certain materials were put into his hands, some correspondence and a life written by the Babylonian Damis, who was himself a disciple of Apollonius. Why then another Life? Because Damis's was doubtless ineptly written and the Life had to be put into proper style to win a respectful hearing by a cultivated audience. One thinks of the literary shortcomings of the Gospel of Mark as compared to the polished style of Luke, who says in his opening verses: "Forasmuch as many have taken in hand to set forth in order a declaration of those things which are most surely believed among us . . . it seemed good to me also . . . to write unto thee. . . ."

In one case we happen to have an original text of the second century B.C. and its revision for a Roman audience at the end of the first century A.D. The *Letter of Aristeas* is a well-written account of the circumstances attending the translation of the Hebrew Scriptures into Greek called the Septuagint. The author wrote the Greek he spoke, very like that of his contemporary, the historian Polybius. When it came time for Josephus to tell the story, in Book xii of his *Antiquities* at the end of the first century A.D., he transcribed it, with classicizing changes, from Aristeas; it is clear that he used no other source. Though he surely knew the Greek of his own day himself, Josephus employed literary assistants, as he himself tells us, to make his work acceptable. The interval of style between the vernacular and the echoes of Thucydides and Sophocles makes the contribution of the literary assistants easy to recognize.

In works like these, attention to style could be justified as giving important material a dignity they would otherwise not have. But style was bound to become an end in itself and to degenerate into a mere display of preciosity. When the correspondence of Marcus Aurelius and the distinguished rhetor Fronto, in Greek and in Latin, was discovered in a palimpsest during the last century, the highest expectations were aroused. Actually all that the philosophic emperor and his teacher have to communicate are stylistic nuggets quite empty of serious meaning. We shall see in the sequel how letters even more empty proliferated in a later century. But the best example of the degree to which style could take precedence over matter is the work of Hermogenes of Tarsus, the most highly regarded teacher of his day of what we should call creative writing. Of Hermogenes we know that he had attained such fame by the age of eighteen that the emperor Marcus Aurelius crossed the sea to hear him lecture, that he lost his mind at the age of twenty-four, so that he could not recognize the works he had written, that he lived on to the age of eighty, and that an autopsy disclosed that his heart was covered with shaggy fur. What all this signifies it is hard to know, except that Hermogenes had become a legend. He was in fact the most revered and the most frequently cited authority in all Byzantine literature. Hermogenes' voluminous writings, still extant, have very little to say to a modern reader; the key to his outlook and teaching is contained in a passage in one of his prefaces, which amounts to this: A mediocrity who takes my course is bound to be a better writer than a genius who does not. To us such a position seems perverse indeed, but it is pathetic rather than shocking. One senses that Hermogenes' audience, in his own day and especially among the Byzantines who studied him, were conscious of their impotence in creativity and so clung desperately to the vessel which was the vehicle of civilization. If the vessel were kept intact it might some day be replenished, as actually happened in several genres during the Renaissance. If the vessel should be allowed to crumble the whole process of civilization would have to begin anew.

The impoverishment of thought to which excessive concern for traditional style might lead is particularly noticeable in the field of philosophy. What had given Greek philosophy its vitality and its continuing freshness was that it was constantly subject to inquiry and change. Sectarians like members of the Pythagorean brotherhood might conclude an argument with *ipse dixit,* but in general no teacher and no school, however high their prestige, could presume to exact acceptance of tenets or outlooks. But in the first century B.C. what philosophers have called the Law of Contradiction fell into abeyance. Study of philosophy became like fundamentalist study of Scripture. There was room for exegesis but none for criticism and innovation; men studied philosophy but abdicated the philosophic quest, which is the untrammeled and unqualified pursuit of truth by intelligence alone and not by received authority. And when philosophy was resuscitated, in the seventeenth century, it was by a resumption of the continuing philosophic dialogue at the point where the Greeks left off.

By the beginning of the Common Era, literary scholarship was endowed with something approaching a religious sanction. Greeks had always regarded literature and philosophy highly and had always respected scholars in these subjects, but when the literary tradition came to be virtually canonized the respect turned to reverence. Even in the *Iliad* (13.355) Zeus's superiority is attributed to the fact that "he was older and so knew more"; now knowing more becomes the principal attribute of deity. Plutarch writes (*Isis and Osiris* 1): "Deity is not blessed by reason of possession of gold and silver, nor strong because of thunder and lightning, but through knowledge and intelligence." When *Paideia* ("Dame Culture") was trying to convert young Lucian to literary culture she said to him (*Enupnion* 12):

It is said that from mortal men some become immortal; and I will effect this for you, for even when you depart from life you shall never cease consorting with the learned and conversing with the best.

The notion that education may procure immortality is not a hyperbole of Lucian's but apparently an accepted article of faith. Tomb inscriptions now record that the deceased was "a man of the Muses," which implied that he merited special consideration in the world to come, and pictures of the blessed dead, in the pseudo-Platonic *Axiochus* and the sixth *Aeneid,* show not only sainted warriors at their sports but also philosophers and poets reading their works to appreciative and respectful throngs.

Incentives so high for loyalty to a style tend not only to calcify it but give it institutional authority. The old separation between traditions of style and traditions of external authority was erased. Stoop-shouldered and myopic scholars who pore over ancient classics in order to win a privileged status in the future world may be poor specimens of the heroic temper, but their studies did keep the vessel in being. Some of its old contents surely touched contemporaries less myopic and less concerned about another world, and some was preserved for new flowering in other centuries. The vessel itself may be as important as its contents, for the vessel itself provides forms in which new content can be generated.

The most devoted guardians of the vessel were the Byzantine Greeks, for whom Hermogenes was the supreme authority in literature and education. The chief object of their education was *hellenismos,* or the preservation of correct Greek style. It is as if they sensed their own impotence in creativity and kept the forms which others might some day fill with more original matter. Their most abundant literary genre was letters, and treatises on letter writing, which include as many as forty model specimens of various types of letters, have come down to us. The subtlety of the distinctions shows how seriously the epistolary art was taken. The first specimen in a treatise ascribed (probably wrongly) to Demetrius of Phalerum is labeled "The Friendly Letter," of which the author says, "The friendly letter is one which purports to be written by a friend to a friend; such are written by persons who are not really friends." The specimen starts, "Though I happen to be separated from you by a great space, it is only my body that is in this case." But nothing in the specimen nor in the hundreds of actual letters which survive is more noteworthy than this sentence in communicating information or thoughts. One wonders that intelligent correspondents had so little to say to each other. The explanation is that the actual message was delivered orally by the messenger who carried the written letter, which was only an obeisance to correct form. And the form did indeed eventually receive worthier content. Libanius, to whom another series of specimen letters was attributed, was much admired by Erasmus, and Erasmus' very numerous and much better letters, and hence the European tradition of elegant epistolography, may be due to the pious preservation of an apparently outworn form.

In drama and romance the efficacy of traditional form is more striking. The drama of the Italian *Rinascimento* was not a continuous development out of antecedent folk plays but directly copied from the ancients. The new playwrights follow Seneca rather than the Greeks and are blind to the spiritual depths we have learned to admire in the Greek; all that they learned was that drama could be a high art worthy of the best efforts of the most artistic writers and the respectful attention of the most accomplished audiences. They learned and perpetuated form, which could then be filled with richer content by the Elizabethans and the Spaniards and others.

The prose romances of the Greeks, written near the beginning of the Christian era, seem trivial. Their characters are two-dimensional, their plots contrived, their substance jejune. But they are beautifully constructed, with beginning, middle, and end, and with several strands of plot held firmly in hand and then combined for a stunning ending. Their artistry must have come as a revelation to people who knew only *Amadis of Gaul* and the enormous and amorphic romances of chivalry which Don Quixote's barber and housekeeper threw on the bonfire. Allusions in several humanist writers show that the Greek romances enjoyed a great vogue. But bits of plot and turns of expression are only incidental; the important lesson, which was carried through the revolutions of centuries and eventually shaped the modern novel, was in style and form.

CHAPTER 9
THE
HELLENISTIC
REVOLUTION

The greatest threat to the survival of essential Greekhood, and the most convincing evidence that humanist culture can survive radical changes in physical environment, in the form of sovereignty and in the climate of ideas, is the revolution of the Hellenistic Age.

The catalyst of the revolution was the conquests of Alexander the Great in the Near and Middle East at the end of the fourth century B.C. Intercourse and cultural interchange between East and West had long antecedents, as we shall observe in the chapter following, but what had been a trickle now swelled into a flood. Geographical, and with them intellectual, horizons were enormously expanded; what had been remote and dim became near and familiar. Old political structures were dissolved and new substituted; the minuscule sovereignties of city-states were engulfed in large political complexes ruled by autocratic kings. There were extensive migrations, especially of Greeks to the East, which made the Hellenistic world a melting pot; not only were the Easterners Hellenized but the Greeks were to some degree orientalized.

The most spectacular of these changes was the new autocracy of kings who claimed to be gods; the most pregnant consequence was the obsolescence of the old city-state. There the individual had enjoyed a high place in the sun. His city offered the individual complete fulfillment and was his spokesman to the outside world. In the Athenian democracy the citizen virtually owned his commonwealth, as a member of an exclusive club owns his clubhouse or a voting stockholder his corporation, and received dividends from the proceeds of his city's imperial holdings not only in the form of handsome public buildings and other amenities but in the form of grain or other bounties. That is why rights of citizenship were so jealously guarded and gave their possessor such high pride. The citizen was an active participant in his city's artistic and intellectual life; tragic poets and artists were his agents and must satisfy his taste. He could be proud of his city's achievements in a way impossible for subjects of autocracies.

But now his insulation was stripped away and his focus dispersed, and he was forced to find a new rationale for his own existence and a new set of attitudes for confronting the world. From a world grown too colossal for the individual to comprehend and indifferent to his own individuality, men turned in upon themselves and sought satisfaction in asserting and probing into their own individuality. The shift of direction is discernible in various forms of expression, in literature and plastic art no less than in philosophy.

From "first philosophies," which had become remote and impractical abstractions, and from speculations on the ideal state, which they could never hope to realize, men turned to ethical systems which might make life tolerable in a terrifyingly large world which reduced them to ciphers. Platonism became academic in the modern as well as the ancient sense; the Middle Academy despaired of all positive knowledge, and would speak only of probability, and the much later Neoplatonists devoted themselves to thaumaturgy and homiletics. Men who would follow specialist disciplines as studied by Aristotle and his successors in the Peripatetic school devoted themselves to even more specialist and professional study at the Library and Museum at Alexandria. Like the Alexandrian poets who wrote elegant miniatures to parade their virtuoso scholarship and techniques, these specialists had little contact with a larger public. The vital teachers who addressed themselves to the spiritual needs of the generality were the Stoics and Epicureans, whose object, as we have seen, each in their own way, was to promote autarky or self-sufficiency by redressing the imbalance between man and his world.

Classical art idealized; Sophocles portrayed men as they should be rather than as they are, and so did portraits in stone also. Figures are idealized, as if they were only a step removed from the gods to whom the ideal was appropriate. People we know to have been old or sick when they were portrayed are shown in their vigorous prime, and there is only the barest suggestion of individuality. Now portraiture becomes painfully realistic; peculiar physical traits and the distortions of pain or passion and the ravages of time are emphasized rather than glossed over. Children and peasant crones are shown in genre scenes, and the style is a flowing realism. When they are overwhelmed by the general, men turn to the particular.

So in literature also the direction is from the generalized to the particular, from the heroic to the bourgeois. Tragedy gives way to New Comedy, probings into questions of man and his fate to concern with establishing identity, marrying, finding a place in the world; men wish to live happily ever after, not to achieve heroism by a glorious death. Formal literature has room not only for bourgeois types, including slaves (as in Menander), but also for peasants (as in Theocritus) and for lower-class urban types (as in Herondas), and even gods and heroes are reduced to the status of ordinary humanity (as in Callimachus or Apollonius). It is true that changes such as these might have developed naturally, for their seeds are already present in Euripides and in Isocrates. What precipitated them and gave them wider currency was the actual blurring of class distinction which came with centralized authoritarian government.

After Alexander's death in 323 B.C. his principal generals continued to hold the areas of which he had made them satraps, but within a dozen years one after another declared himself king and established a dynasty, the Antigonids in old Greece, the Ptolemies in Egypt, and the Seleucids in Asia as far as India. Though the kings were Macedonian by race they asserted their authority as the legitimate successors of the native dynasties, a claim defensible only for the Antigonids. Monarchy was therefore orientalized, which is to say, made unlimited; the Pharaohs had claimed personal divinity, the Eastern kings had claimed to be exclusive agents of divinity, and soon the kings in Macedonia engineered deification for themselves also.

In a polytheism with anthropomorphic gods deification is of course not so blasphemous as it might appear to monotheists with a conception of a transcendent deity. The significance was political rather than religious; a vote of deification, spontaneous or engineered, was merely an expression of gratitude for favors received, or favors hoped for. There was even some precedent: great benefactors of humanity had been traditionally heroized, though this honor could be conferred only after death. Legend recorded that certain authentic deities, notably Heracles and Dionysus, had been living mortals when they were made gods. Furthermore Euhemerus had suggested that all the Olympians, including Zeus himself, had once been mortals and had received divinity in recognition of remarkable services to mankind; Euhemerism had a considerable vogue and was even propagated by the Latin poet Ennius. The political motivation of deification is shown by its adaptation in Rome. At first Roman emperors were deified only after death, if their reigns were considered benevolent; one like Caligula who claimed divine honors in his lifetime was considered mad. But Rome itself was deified, and temples to Rome were erected, in the eastern half of the empire, significantly, to give a religious basis and sanction to the demands of national discipline. The motive of the deification of Hellenistic kings was obviously analogous. In the Greek world thoughtful men were nevertheless exercised to find a rationale for the power of a king. Philosophers of several schools wrote treatises "On Kingship" to show why legislative power could be transferred from a popular assembly to an individual and how the unexampled concentration of authority in the person of a king could be justified. The usual solution, based ultimately on Plato, was that the king was *nomos empsychos,* "law incarnate," so that his every utterance had legal validity.

Oriental kingship meant exploitation of the populace, not service to it, and in this respect the Macedonian kings were efficient followers of the native dynasties from which they claimed legitimate succession. To secure loyalty and efficiency they required Greeks (or later thoroughly Hellenized natives) for army and administration, and so went to great pains and expense to encourage Greek immigration. Besides the depressed economic state of Greece there were political and other reasons why many Greeks should go abroad to seek their fortunes, and there was a large migration to the newly opened lands, how large it is difficult to estimate. But however large, the newcomers must have remained a minority, even in localities to which they gave Greek names. The remarkable thing is that, being a minority, they resisted assimilation to the majority and even succeeded in attracting the natives to Greek speech and Greek ways.

The rapid Hellenization of the East is the most impressive practical achievement of Greekhood. The Greeks did not merely transfer their culture to a continent sparsely occupied by primitive natives, as English settlers did in America; the natives among whom the Greeks settled were numerous and themselves heirs to cultural traditions from which the ancestors of the Greeks had learned. Rather the Greeks were in the position of later non-English immigrants to America, who have been thoroughly integrated with the English-speaking majority. What makes the Greek experience remarkable is that instead of being assimilated to the established culture, as the American pattern suggests they might have been, they spread their own culture among the natives, and not so much by an organized program of cultural imperialism (though the authorities countenanced and sometimes promoted Hellenization) as by the example set by their own adherence to Greek ways.

The unit of administration in the newly formed monarchies was the city, and the regular device for expanding and implementing the rule of the central government was establishment of cities of the Greek pattern. These might be new foundations, perhaps originally military colonies, but were usually reorganizations superimposed on a native village or combination of villages. Alexandria in Egypt and Antioch in Syria, which developed into the greatest of Hellenistic metropolises, started their careers in this way, but there was a great proliferation of lesser cities, several bearing the name of Alexandria (after Alexander the Great) or of Antioch (most Seleucid kings were named Antiochus). In Greek terminology a concentration of population, no matter how large, was only a village unless it possessed certain organs of public life which made it a *polis*. Among the essentials were a council, an assembly, elected magistrates, a fiscal system, and certain urban amenities, including a *gymnasion*. The cities not only facilitated the business of the central government, including the collection of taxes, but provided a reservoir of personnel with Greek training for the military and other needs of the central government. But no pressure needed to be applied to a native community to become a *polis;* on the contrary, even populous and prosperous native communities were so eager to acquire the advantages and prestige of becoming a *polis* that they were willing to pay for the privilege. For a time Jerusalem itself seems to have been a *polis,* under the name of Antioch.

Just as the new age stripped the insulation from the city-states of Greece so it stripped the insulation from the peoples of the East also. Their governmental structures had collapsed, and history had shown that when a sovereignty collapsed, there collapsed with it the religious and social usages of which the sovereignty had been patron and which it enjoined. Not only were the old ways deprived of their authority but their very validity was put into question by the mere presence of the Greeks. Here were newcomers whose very different traditions made them gayer and freer and quicker, whose technology was superior, and, most impressive of all, who were successful. Their clothing and their buildings, their manners and their arts, seemed attractive, and the amenities of their cities sophisticated and agreeable. Moreover there were potent practical considerations to motivate emulation of the Greeks. A native who desired to enter government service or army or large-scale commerce or who merely had social ambitions would almost be bound to Hellenize. And so at least upper-class natives learned to speak Greek and adopted Greek names—at least for public or official purposes; they might bear native names and speak the vernacular at home or among intimates.

Membership in council or assembly was limited to those who had attended the *gymnasion;* that is why admission to the *gymnasion* was sometimes so rigorously limited, as in Alexandria. But very many natives did receive Greek education; the numerous and large theaters scattered all over the Hellenistic world, even as far as Babylon, could not have been filled by Greeks alone. And they read Greek books, and eventually wrote them. The books they wrote in their own languages to glorify their own past not only followed Greek literary modes but exhibited Greek outlooks. They saw themselves through Greek lenses and measured themselves by Greek standards; their object was not to polemicize against the Greeks but rather to show that their own history and traditions made them worthy of acceptance into the Greek world. Presently they wrote Greek books also, and these found their place in the general literary stream.

And the Greek world was ready to receive them as equals. Isocrates had said that a man with a Greek education is Greek, the Cynics and Stoics had taught the equality of all people, and the Epicurean evangel was addressed to Greeks and non-Greeks alike. That the survival of Greekhood and not racial clannishness was the paramount consideration of the Greeks is shown by their marriages. In the farther reaches of the East, where Greeks were few and their Greekhood therefore in danger of being diluted, Greeks avoided intermarriage with non-Greeks, whereas in the westerly portions where Greeks were numerous and there was no such danger, Greeks intermarried freely. Non-Greek spouses were assimilated to Greekhood, not the other way around.

Religion was not the bar to intercourse which we might expect. Polytheisms are naturally not exclusive; adherence to one set of beliefs does not imply denial of the validity of a different set of beliefs held by others. Greek deities were local rather than universal. It was right for a Greek away from home to honor the deities and observe the cult usages of the place of his sojourn, with no feeling that he was being remiss in neglecting his own religious obligations. If Zeus was the chief deity among the Greeks they could conceive of the chief deity of another people as being his equivalent, and were ready to worship him under his local name and according to local usages. Greeks could join in the worship of the Syrian Lord of Heaven and Syrians in the worship of Zeus without either party feeling that it had betrayed its sanctities.

This latitudinarianism led to various syncretisms, some quite peculiar. The cult of Sarapis was actually fabricated in the third century B.C., and Sarapis purposefully made to combine the characteristics and functions of several pre-existent deities, Greek and Egyptian. Sarapis enjoyed a wide vogue, especially in cosmopolitan centers, particularly on the island of Delos, which were meeting places of men of different traditions. Sarapis was supplanted by the religion of Isis, which offered greater emotional satisfaction and encouraged a higher ethical code. The *Isis and Osiris* of Plutarch, who was notably loyal to Greekhood and notably devout, demonstrates that the alien gods are in fact Egyptian manifestations of Greek deities and that the observances required by them, which might seem rank superstition to Greeks, were in fact rich in spiritual symbolism of universal validity. But the apologetic is on behalf of the Egyptians, not the Greeks. The Greeks are still the unquestioned standards, and other peoples are judged (and in the Hellenistic world judged themselves) according as they approached or deviated from the Greek norm.

The only peoples who insisted on the exclusive truth of their religions (though both were to some degree products of syncretism) and who rejected alien cults were the Persians and the Hebrews. Of the reactions of the latter we are better informed, chiefly through the Apocrypha and in particular the Books of the Maccabees. It was to preserve the integrity of their religious practices that the Maccabees revolted against Antiochus. But it should be noticed that the insurrection was precipitated by the rivalry of two claimants for the high priesthood, each of whom bore a Greek name and was thoroughly Hellenized, and that the priests and upper classes were quite willing to wear Greek costume and attend the *gymnasion* (concealing the evidence of circumcision by painful surgery) and to countenance the worship of the "abomination of desolation" which had been set up in the Temple. After the insurrection succeeded the Hasmonean rulers proved as philhellene as other princes in the Hellenistic world, and no more spiritual or humane. Not only in the more numerous diaspora but in Palestine itself Jews spoke Greek and read Greek books, used Greek patterns of architecture and decoration, dressed and dined in the Greek manner. Like other non-Greeks in the Hellenistic world they contributed to the Greek cultural stream also, as we shall see in the chapter following.

We know that books written by other non-Greeks, even when they were intended to glorify native tradition, were deeply influenced by Hellenism. It is perhaps more striking that the extant books of the Apocrypha and so-called Pseudepigrapha, written during the intertestamentary period and calculated to strengthen Jewish pieties, are so deeply tinged with Greek outlooks and Greek modes of thought and expression. The Apocryphal Books of the Maccabees faithfully follow the prescriptions of Hellenistic historiography. The Wisdom of Solomon is influenced by the form of the Cynic-Stoic diatribe. The tone of Ecclesiasticus, or the Wisdom of Sirach, is thoroughly Attic. For instance, if a man falls sick he should pray and repent—but remember to call a physician. Ecclesiasticus is concerned for the orderly functioning of society and for specialization and competence among craftsmen. The familiar eulogy of famous men recognizes not only effective administrators, counselors, and orators, but also "such as found out musical tunes and recited verses in writing." The Book of Judith is a palpable fiction calculated to reinforce lessons of piety. The first portion is obviously influenced by Herodotus's classic account of the apparently irresistible advance of a huge Oriental host against a spiritual elect; the telltale "earth and water" which the tyrant demands as token of submission is straight out of Herodotus. The deliverance of the spiritual elect after a wait of five days, when it had been cut off from water, follows a similar story inscribed on stone at Lindos on the island of Rhodes. Instead of the goddess Athena the agent of deliverance here is the virtuous Judith. The central episode of her encounter with Holofernes breathes the atmosphere of Greek romance.

Among the books of the noncanonical Pseudepigrapha the most artistic and the most thoroughly Greek in form is the Fourth Book of the Maccabees. The subject is the martyrdom of the aged Eleazar and of Hannah's seven sons. Form and content are deeply influenced by Greek tragedy and Greek philosophy. The persecuting king uses Stoic arguments, and those of Eleazar are Platonist, drawn largely from the *Gorgias*. The scene is typical of tragedy, and the action is carried forward by dialogue. The brothers are several times referred to as a "chorus," and there is an echo of a pathetic passage in Euripides' *Trojan Women*. Not only could so pious an author show mastery of Greek style and Greek literature, but he could assume that his large audience was prepared to appreciate his learning and his modes of argumentation. Other works of the intertestamentary period are tinged with if less thoroughly steeped in Hellenism. The Judaism out of which Christianity grew was already Hellenized, and though Christianity was hostile to Hellenism it itself carried a large measure of Hellenism forward.

More striking than these instances from the little-read intertestamentary writings are the effects of Hellenism discernible in later books of the Old Testament canon proper. The form and content of the Book of Job, it has been plausibly argued, suggest that its author was acquainted with Greek tragedy. Only in Job, among the Old Testament books, God is not the patron of a peculiar people; only here is an extensive and probing dialogue distributed among a cast of characters, only here is the justice of God examined and questioned unflinchingly. Like the Greek authors of tragedy, the author of Job has expanded an ancient myth and clothed it in noble poetry to ponder on man's relations to the divine. Ecclesiastes surely reflects the philosophic climate of the Hellenistic Age, mainly Epicurean but in part also Stoic. Canticles (in which the word God occurs only in an epithet to characterize the intensity of the flame of love) shows affinities with Hellenistic love poetry in form as well as content. Other less striking examples could be cited, but these are sufficient to show how peoples who abhorred Hellenism were unwitting carriers of a certain measure of Greek style.

If some stubborn non-Greeks refused to acknowledge that they had received cultural benefits from the Greeks (most non-Greeks were very ready to acknowledge that they had and even called themselves "barbarians") the later Greeks claimed credit for their cultural evangel. Towards the end of the first century A.D. the youthful Plutarch has this to say in an essay *On the Fortune of Alexander* (328 f.); the context is an argument that Alexander was a more effective teacher than the professed philosophers:

When Alexander civilized Asia Homer became common reading, and the sons of Persians, Susianians, and Gedrosians learned to intone the tragedies of Sophocles and Euripides. And although Socrates when tried on the charge of introducing foreign deities lost his cause to the informers who infested Athens, yet through Alexander Bactria and the Caucasus learned to revere the gods of the Greeks. Plato wrote a book on the ideal state, but because of its forbidding character he could not persuade anyone to adopt it; but Alexander established more than seventy cities among savage tribes, and sowed all Asia with Grecian magistracies, and thus overcame its uncivilized and brutish manner of living. Although few of us read Plato's *Laws*, yet hundreds of thousands have made use of Alexander's laws and continue to use them. Those who were vanquished by Alexander are happier than those who escaped his hand, for these had no one to put an end to the wretchedness of their existence, while the victor compelled those others to lead a happy life. . . . Alexander's new subjects would not have been civilized had they not been vanquished; Egypt would not have its Alexandria, nor Mesopotamia its Seleuceia, nor Sogdiana its Prophthasia, nor India its Bucephalia, nor the Caucasus the Greek City; for by the founding of cities in these places savagery was extinguished and the worse element, gaining familiarity with the better, changed under its influence. If, then, philosophers take the greatest pride in civilizing and rendering adaptable the intractable and untutored elements in human character, and if Alexander has been shown to have changed the savage natures of countless tribes, it is with good reason that he should be regarded as a very great philosopher.

(Translated by F. C. BABBITT)

Plutarch is speaking only of the East; a century before, Roman Horace had said "Captive Greece captivated its captors."

CHAPTER 10
THE EASTERN INGREDIENT

Monuments of the ancient Near and Middle East displayed in a museum seem alien and puzzling; they enlarge the spectator's experience, but they can also be frightening. As he strolls on to exhibits from classical Greece his sympathies are awakened and his appreciation heightened. These are not exotic but reflect the thought and taste of his own cultural ancestors. Ancestors but not contemporaries: their remote austerity may overawe him and make him uneasy. But as he moves on to the products of the Hellenistic Age he recognizes his own world; Greece in the Hellenistic Age is hardly more alien than a modern foreign country which shares the European tradition is alien. The foundations of European culture, in ethics as in art, were indeed laid by the classical Greeks; but the developed structure, with its diminutions and enlargements, which the Romans adapted and transmitted to the countries of Europe, is first recognizable in the Hellenistic Age. The differences from the old are of course largely due to historical development, but this was accelerated and guided by direct influences from the East, and received its particular conformation by the less tangible working of an Eastern leaven. In order to understand the new directions, and especially the shift in attitudes to authority and tradition and its preservation, we must seek to assess the influences from the East.

Cultural interchange was not so difficult in the Hellenistic Age as it might have been with remoter parts of the East. Whether because they represent divergent channels from common cultural sources or, far more likely, because of direct contacts, there are perceptible affinities between Greece and the East from the very earliest times. Did Orphic ideas of the duality of body and soul originate in Greece or in Mesopotamia? Are the Hittite parallels to the castration of Ouranos and the succession of Cronus accidental? Does Homeric epic owe anything to the form and objective and atmosphere of the Gilgamesh epic? Is elegy originally Phrygian? Were not the Ionian pre-Socratics who were ultimately responsible for the Greek enlightenment heirs to an Eastern tradition? Even in the later confrontation between Greek and Judeo-Christian tradition there is a sense that the principals are not wholly alien to one another but in a manner siblings—and therefore more violent in their opposition.

In recorded history the Greeks' first major contact with the East was in the Persian Wars, but for more than a century before, Greeks had carried on trade with the East and had served as mercenary soldiers and in other capacities in Hither Asia and in Egypt. Down to the period of the Persian Wars there is no evidence of Greek contempt for Easterners. In the *Iliad* Trojan language, religion, and outlooks are not different from Greek, and in early vase paintings Trojan warriors are represented as Ionian hoplites. *Barbaros* has no pejorative connotation even in Herodotus; the word simply means "not Greek-speaking," and *barbaroi* are not despised as such. Both Herodotus and Aeschylus, in their accounts of the Persians, show the greatest respect for their chivalry and discipline and high courtesy.

It was only after the repulse of the Persian invasions, when Greek self-awareness was accentuated, as might be expected, that "barbarian" took on pejorative connotations. Vase paintings now represent the Oriental as effeminate and finicky, and literature as unreliable and cowardly and servile. Though the Persians did not again invade

Greece they continued to affect Greek politics, mainly by subsidizing the weaker side in any intestine struggle. The easy parade of Greek military superiority in the march of the ten thousand Greek mercenaries into the Asian interior (about 401 B.C.) of which Xenophon tells in his *Anabasis* revealed the weakness of the Persian dominion. Isocrates' suggestion that the Greeks unite for a crusade against the East was not impractically visionary. After Philip of Macedon had subdued all of Greece, his son Alexander, looking for new worlds to conquer, did in fact annihilate Persian rule, which covered the entire Near and Middle East, including Egypt, and himself became master of the huge conglomerate and even extended it to the Indus. After his death, as has been described above, his generals divided his realm into disparate entities.

Alexander himself assented to divinization, which was an essential, in his situation, to enhance prestige and authority. But he could jest about it; once when he was wounded he remarked to his friends, "It's blood, you see, not ichor," and he chafed at hyperbolic adulation. His way was not the Oriental conception of kingship, where the king was a superior being and all lesser men were his servants, but the Macedonian, where the king was *primus inter pares,* first among equals, or the Stoic, where the king was not the master but the minister of his people. A prime object of his ministry was to fuse all peoples, on terms of equality, into a single brotherhood. Philosophically the ground had been prepared; for a century enlightened Greeks had taught the equality of all men, and Isocrates had said that Greek style was a matter not of race but of education.

It was natural for a Greek, whether Isocrates or Alexander's generals or non-Greeks of any period who shared the outlooks of Greekhood, to conceive of fusion as assimilation to Greek modes, and from the viewpoint of Hellenism and its heirs the Greek element was in fact overwhelmingly predominant. But the traffic was not all one way. The most significant change brought by the counter-traffic was the transfer of political authority to autocracy supported by religious sanctions which might claim direction over all aspects of private as well as public life. Other changes are somehow related to this basic one. Attitudes to tradition shifted; where there had been relative indifference to traditions of political and religious institutions while those of humanist style had been scrupulously maintained, now the authority of formal institutions became absolute and that of humanist style relatively relaxed. That it was maintained at all shows the vitality of essential Greekhood and suggests that humanist style might again survive the exigencies of environmental changes.

The congeries of peoples which comprised the Persian empire included the civilizations of Anatolia as well as Egypt, which had attained a very high level of civilization as far back as the third millennium B.C. Between then and the time of their incorporation into the Persian Empire they had undergone numerous vicissitudes, including changes of sovereignty and of language. Cultural survivals transcending these changes are different in techniques and results from the survival of Hellenism, but are very impressive nevertheless. The Assyrian version of the Gilgamesh epic, which is obviously the source for the Biblical story of the Deluge, is more than a millennium later than the Babylonian version and but little changed in substance. Much of the civil legislation of the Pentateuch similarly derives from the Babylonian code of Hammurabi over a similar interval of time. Puzzling details in the narratives of the patriarchs, like Abraham's calling his wife his sister, which is ethically questionable in the Biblical context, are now shown to be accurate if anachronistic echoes of actual Hurrian usages centuries before. The Ugaritic writings which are nearer the Biblical in time but still centuries removed, show striking similarities to the language, imagery, rhythms, and to a degree the thought of prophets and Psalms. In the centuries during which the Biblical books were written, the angelology, dualism of body and soul, meticulous prescriptions for sacrificial ritual, show obvious Persian elements acquired during the Babylonian exile in the sixth century B.C. On the history and civilization of Persia itself Herodotus provides illuminating passages, though he somewhat strangely makes no mention of Zoroastrianism.

When the archaeology of the more ancient Near East came to be studied critically, about a century ago, it was essentially a department of Biblical research, its motive being to illuminate the Biblical accounts and to demonstrate (or alternatively to impugn) their veracity. In our own time materials for investigation, including substantial bodies of literature, have become abundant enough to justify the study of the Near East for its own sake as a significant chapter, or rather volume, in man's cultural history. The balances are so shifted that, except for those specifically concerned with Bible, Biblical archaeology is contributory to pre- and extra-Biblical, not the other way around.

And yet if our object is to understand the effects of Eastern ingredients upon the cultural stream which emanates from the Greeks, it is correct as well as convenient to make the Bible represent the East, for besides its own very great contributions it did subsume the elements of ancient thought that have affected the general cultural stream and it was the means by which these elements were enabled to exercise their effects. It was the complex of ideas called Hellenism and the complex of ideas represented by the Bible, not their several antecedents, which had to confront one another and come to terms with one another. Each proved elastic enough to be substantially influenced by the other, and, perhaps for that reason, both were able to survive. Both survivals are alike remarkable for having transcended loss of political sovereignty; except as it was absorbed in one or the other no other ancient culture survived the sovereignty which had fostered it as a recognizable and living entity.

The books in the Biblical canon are a deliberate and purposeful selection out of a large body of literature that must have been available.The rationale of the selection is that all somehow illuminate the relations of God, who is of course one and omnipotent, with his chosen people. The basis of the relationship is a covenant, entered into by Abraham on behalf of all his posterity, which specified the role of both parties. A passage like Leviticus 26 lists the blessings of prosperity that will accrue "If ye walk in my statutes, and keep my commandments, and do them" and the disasters "if ye will not for all this hearken unto me, but walk contrary unto me." The history set forth in the Bible is a demonstration of the operation of the covenant. The reforms of King Josiah in 621 B.C. gave new emphasis to the idea of the covenant and gave it a firm organizational structure by prescribing a sole and central sanctuary to regulate the religious life of the whole people. The book whose "discovery" instigated the reform was Deuteronomy, and it is thought that justifications and prescriptions for a central sanctuary even in earlier books owe their presence there to the reforms of Josiah.

In course of time the implications of the covenant might be spiritualized or extended, but its central thesis was never questioned. The prophets urge greater spirituality and greater universality, but even when knowledge of God shall cover the earth as the waters cover the sea, instruction will still go forth from Zion and the word of God from Jerusalem. When later pietist groups like the Essenes or the Qumran sectarians became ascetics and mystics, they did not negate the covenant but performed the obligations it entailed more adequately; they might deplore the worldliness of contemporary leaders but they did not question the validity of the establishment. Pharisees might devise new legislation or mitigate the old in order to meet new needs or more refined sensibilities, but they based their enactments not on a rejection of Scripture but on sanctioned reinterpretation of it; Scripture continued to be the authoritative code of the covenant. Even Christianity, which, especially in its antinomian aspects, is the most deviationist of all, acknowledged and built upon the doctrine of the covenant of which it was the "fulfillment." Its organization and direction of the religious sphere was the most ramified and the most solid of all.

Classical Greece has nothing like a covenant and its ramifications to show, and it is therefore the more remarkable that classical Rome, which learned even political theory from the Greeks, does have something very similar. The charter of Rome, it has been suggested above, is its divinely directed history, just as the history told in the Old Testament was the national charter of the Hebrews, and the quasi-scripture which set that history forth is the *Aeneid*. The story which the *Aeneid* tells is in brief as follows. Troy had been founded by the Latin Dardanus, and so the Trojans were in fact Italians who had sojourned for some centuries in what was to prove a temporary domicile; their true home, their promised land, was Italy. After a national humiliation a leader divinely appointed (Aeneas was the son of Venus, who had preserved him, alone of the greater Trojan chieftains, through the Trojan War) receives a mission to carry the remnants of the Trojans and the national religious emblems back to Italy and found a state there. He conducts his people by a roundabout route, in the course of which they are subjected to many trials and to the temptation to give their mission up, but after a hard struggle Aeneas succeeds in establishing his people in Italy and so in fulfilling the divine promise. Repeatedly there are promises of a glorious and endless future and reminders that the Romans must always be mindful of their mission and serve it faithfully. Aeneas is not obsessed with self like Achilles, but a disciplined instrument of destiny. His followers are called Aeneadae, children of Aeneas—the Greeks are never called children of Achilles or Odysseus—and Aeneas himself must subsume all the virtues his descendants are to show and must prove the worthy progenitor of the family which will bear rule when the Romans renew allegiance to their mission. We need not infer that Vergil borrowed from Exodus, but he did breathe a climate different from that of classical Greece. The influences of the Vergilian premises upon the political climate of Europe, in turn, are incalculable. Medieval theorists may sometimes cite the houses of David and the Maccabees for the divinity that hedges a king, but the operative element in naturalizing the conviction was not Biblical but Vergilian.

The major increments from the East, then, and the most radical, were the notions not only of an authoritarian and centralized kingship but also of an authoritarian and centralized religious establishment which was commonly associated if not identical with royal authority in the countries of the Near and Middle East. It was with these and the outlooks they generated that the humanist tradition had to come to terms, and the humanist tradition with which the notion of centralized political authority had to come to terms for both to survive as ingredients of the Hellenistic amalgam which determined the civilization of Europe. The interval between the two was not wholly unbridgeable. Though the Greeks might chafe at monarchy and when it did exist tend to limit its powers (the kings of Sparta were mere figureheads) they were not unacquainted with the institution. And though they had no central religious authority they were deeply aware of religion, and sometimes on a high philosophical level; there is scarcely a page of classical Greek poetry which does not touch upon religion. On the other hand, a divinely ordained autocracy need not cancel the values of human dignity; if all men are servants of God they are equal, and not servants one of another. Nor was the East indifferent to aesthetic values. The noble poetry of the prophets, to say nothing of its Ugaritic prototypes or of Gilgamesh, shows a lively concern with literary artistry.

In the event, to put the matter briefly for the present, Christianity itself digested much of the humanistic tradition and was itself the instrument for transmitting so much of it as it could assimilate. The Greek Fathers in particular generally possessed broad secular learning, and by the sixth century, when the schools of philosophy were closed, important elements of the humanist tradition were fully integrated into the Christian stream. The Roman Fathers were initially more reluctant to embrace secular learning, but then Jerome prescribed that the potential snare might be introduced into Christianity "with her head shaven and her nails pared" like the gentile captive in Deuteronomy 22.12, and Augustine, who confesses an early passion for pagan literature, advises that "the Egyptians should be spoiled" for the benefit of the Church.

Of Eastern influence upon the West the most telling example is the political and religious organization of the Roman Empire. The polity of the early royal period and the republic which followed it is roughly analogous to the polities of Greece, as we should expect of cognate peoples. Except that its language was Latin Rome was clearly a cultural province of Greece—not of the remote classical Greece but of the contemporary Hellenistic complex. It was the Eastern ingredient of that complex that seems to have suggested the pattern of the Empire. The Romans had been divinely chosen as the bearers of a mission, had been providentially guided to their promised land, given rulers who were the agents of that providence and who, like the Hellenistic monarchs, assumed divine status.

The conviction that providence would always make Rome successful (in Livy reverses are chastisement for backsliding or a device to encourage military prowess) and would be without end (*imperium sine fine dedi,* in Vergil's words) illustrates another deviation from Greek thought. A common Greek view was that history proceeded not in a steady linear progression but in recurrent cycles. This is the basis of Plato's *Timaeus,* which speaks of a former (and better organized) Athens which flourished ages before the Athens he knew, and of the millennial conflagrations and renewals which the Stoics and others posited. At the destruction of Carthage, when Rome was apparently secure forever, its destroyer Scipio Aemilianus could foresee that Rome too would fall, and murmured Hector's lines (*Iliad* 6.448):

> There will come a day when sacred Ilion shall perish,
> And Priam, and the people of Priam.

That was because Scipio was steeped in Greek literature and philosophy. Perhaps Ecclesiastes (1.9) was similarly influenced by Greek ideas: "The thing that hath been, it is that which shall be; and that which is done is that which shall be done; and there is no new thing under the sun." Where history is providentially directed it proceeds forward in a direct line to some final consummation. The dominance of this view in later speculation is one, and perhaps a minor, outgrowth of the Eastern strand in Hellenistic thought.

Cultural interchange between East and West operated like a pendulum. A Western element might be deposited in the East, transformed, and then brought back to the West in its altered form. Books written in the East according to the newly acquired Greek mode were first addressed to native audiences, but soon such books written in Greek joined the main stream of Hellenistic literature. The drive to righteousness of Easterners who embraced Stoicism or the sensuousness of a Meleager or the popular homilies of Cynic teachers, all of which are to some extent innovations in Greek, may have received their character from the non-Greek antecedents of their authors. Generally speaking, matter from the West had its initial effect upon the upper classes of the East, from which it gradually seeped downward, whereas matter from the East affected the lower classes in the West, from which it gradually rose upward. The result of the process, by the early centuries of Christianity, was an amalgam; culturally if not politically the Stoic or Alexander's ideal of an *oikoumene* was close to realization. But the dominant tone and style of the amalgam were Greek.

CHAPTER 11
ROMAN STYLE

Rome was a highly organized and powerful institution, but Rome was also extremely tenacious of style. Where Greece shows a tension between the authority of institutions and the authority of style, in Rome the institution itself was an expression of style and its chief guardian.

The thousand-year history of Rome shows a stability unexampled in Europe; the ideals of sobriety and dignity, integrity and patriotic devotion, which the Romans believed had animated their founding fathers they held in reverence throughout their history, and the substance of their government underwent radical changes with the minimum disturbance to traditional forms. The authority of government was conceived of as an abstraction called *imperium*. When the early monarchy, traditionally founded in 754 B.C., gave way to the Republic in 510, the *imperium* was simply transferred from the king to two elected consuls with annual tenure, but the machinery of government remained the same. The Senate had been a council of elders who advised the king; under the Republic the Senate's responsibilities increased greatly, but constitutionally it remained an advisory rather than a legislative body. The Republican government persisted long after it had become unworkable. When Rome had come to dominate Italy and was waging war across the seas, governors of remote areas who were in command of armies and whose terms of office were necessarily extended grew more powerful than the government in the capital, and individual rivalries for wealth and power caused disorders. When Julius Caesar realistically took power into his own hands, disregarding the ancient forms, he was assassinated. The Empire which Augustus then founded was in fact far more authoritarian, but his boast of having restored the Republic is correct so far as outward forms are concerned. Though the seat of power shifted, to the outward eye Senate and consuls and other magistrates continued to function as they had always done; Augustus kept power in his own hands by keeping the relatively minor office of tribune, which enabled him to exercise the veto, and the governorship of provinces which required military establishments, in his own hands. Again adherence to traditional but outworn forms had its price. The fiction that the emperor was not really an emperor prevented regular dynastic succession, so that there was danger of bloody competition at the death of each emperor, and for a time the choice was made by the elite garrison in Rome called praetorian guards. Emperors who wished to designate their successors did so by adopting them, which gave them control of the imperial treasury, and appointing them to such offices as would make their succession automatic. Throughout Roman life, as in Roman law, the device of legal fictions to maintain traditions which might otherwise collapse was common.

Piety to ancient usages was paralleled by piety, amounting almost to ancestor worship, to ancient personages. In the ornamental but little-used formal parlor of a Roman of the ruling class there was a cabinet which contained the death masks of his ancestors who had held high office, and on the occasion of a funeral professional actors wearing these masks marched in the cortège. All of life was under the surveillance of the worthies of the past; literature and art glorified them in ways alien to the Greek. Conservatism is indicated even in costume; the formal togas in portrait statues centuries apart in time differ little from one another. It was quite fitting for the Romans to be referred to as *gens togata,* for a man wearing a toga cannot hurry and cannot mince.

Attitudes to religion are significant and revealing. Originally, and throughout the countryside, the Roman religion was a simple and amiable animism. There were numerous numina or spirits, not in human form, who presided over various spheres—beginnings, boundaries, the pantry, the bedroom, various processes in agriculture, various handicrafts. When Greek literature and art came to be imported wholesale, Greek gods too came to Rome. Some were identified with similar Roman numina; Venus, for example, who had been a numen of "charm," took on not only the form but the attributes and the mythology of Aphrodite. But the official pantheon was regarded with little warmth and exercised very little of what we should think of as religious influence. Their cults, tended by professional priests, were rather like the sanitation or fire department a modern municipality maintains. The individual citizen does not have the appliances and expertise to guard against epidemics or fire, and so the municipality relieves him of any attention to these dangers. The colleges of priests were in effect fashionable and luxurious dining clubs; one priest could not meet another on the Sacred Way, it was said, without a smile and a wink.

But for the interests of the state, which were paramount, religion had practical usefulness in ensuring public probity and discipline. Indeed Polybius, the shrewd Greek historian of Rome, thinks it was maintained, if not invented, for the express purpose (6.56):

But the quality in which the Roman commonwealth is most distinctly superior is in my opinion the nature of their religious convictions. I believe that it is the very thing which among other peoples is an object of reproach, I mean superstition, which maintains the cohesion of the Roman State. These matters are clothed in such pomp and introduced to such an extent into their public and private life that nothing could exceed it, a fact which will surprise many. My own opinion at least is that they have adopted this course for the sake of the common people. It is a course which perhaps would not have been necessary had it been possible to form a state composed of wise men, but as every multitude is fickle, full of lawless desires, unreasoned passion, and violent anger, the multitude must be held in by invisible terrors and such-like pageantry. For this reason I think, not that the ancients acted rashly and at haphazard in introducing among the people notions concerning the gods and beliefs in the terrors of hell, but that the moderns are most rash and foolish in banishing such beliefs. The consequence is that among the Greeks, apart from other things, members of the government, if they are entrusted with no more than a talent, though they have ten copyists and as many seals and twice as many witnesses, cannot keep their faith; whereas among the Romans those who as magistrates and legates are dealing with large sums of money maintain correct conduct just because they have pledged their faith by oath. Whereas elsewhere it is a rare thing to find a man who keeps his hands off public money, and whose record is clean in this respect, among the Romans one rarely comes across a man who has been detected in such conduct.

(*Translated by* W. B. PATON)

Perhaps Polybius is cynical, but the thoroughly Roman Cicero (in his *Laws*), a century later, speaks of the practical efficacy of inculcating religious beliefs:

So in the very beginning we must persuade our citizens that the gods are the lords and rulers of all things, and that what is done is done by their will and authority; that they are likewise great benefactors of man, observing the character of every individual, what he does, of what wrong he is guilty, and with what intentions and with what piety he fulfills his religious duties; and that they take note of the pious and the impious. For surely minds which are imbued with such ideas will not fail to form true and useful opinions.

(*Translated by* C. W. KEYES)

To purists the manipulation of religion for practical ends may seem abhorrent, but to the Romans, as to Neoplatonists who practiced thaumaturgy to promote genuine spirituality, their exploitation of credulity was in the service of genuine religious feelings, for the real object of their religion was Rome itself. Probably this had always been the case to a considerable degree, but it was Augustus who made the religion of Rome into a program, and he propagated and exploited it with consummate skill. The *Aeneid*, written under his sponsorship, provides a virtual scripture for the cult. It records Rome's sacred origins and early history, glorifies its saints, authorizes the institution of the Empire, defines the duties of its citizens, and promises a glorious and unending future. The prose history of Livy, also a protégé of Augustus, is similar in character and similarly attributes Rome's origin and destiny to divine providence. What is of special interest here is that Livy himself apparently has rationalist reservations concerning the literal truth of the stories of Rome's origins but insists that they must be propagated nevertheless; in his Preface he says: "And if license is allowed any nation to exalt its inception and make the gods its sponsors, so towering is the military glory of Rome that when it avows that Mars himself was its father and the father of its founder, the races of mankind can submit to the claim with as little qualm as they submit to Rome's dominion." Traditional style is more important and communicates a truer image than does reality.

The ancient history of Rome was recounted not only to show the operation of its destiny but as background for the great personages who symbolized it. In the *Aeneid* (Book 6), whose fictive date is the twelfth century B.C., Aeneas is shown a parade of the worthies who would make Rome great, and he carries their likenesses on his divinely made shield. Livy provides a virtual hagiology of Rome's saints, who embody the ideal image of Rome. For homespun virtue rising to the call of duty Cincinnatus is the prototype. Clad in a smock he was hoeing his field when he was summoned to save the state; he put on his toga, did his public duty, and then returned to his smock and hoe. High principles (and the advantage they bring) are illustrated in the campaign against Falerii. On the pretense of a long walk a Faliscan schoolmaster brought the children of the most influential Faliscans into the Roman camp, expecting gratitude for causing the Faliscans to surrender. But the Roman Camillus said:

"Neither the people to whom you bring this blackguard's gift, you blackguard, nor their general is of your stripe. With the Faliscans we have no fellowship founded on men's covenants, but there is and there will continue to be between us the fellowship implanted by nature. War as well as peace has its laws, and we wage it with justice as well as vigor. Our arms we bear not against children, who are spared even when cities are stormed, but against men armed like ourselves, who attacked our camp at Veii without provocation. You have conquered them, as you think, by a scoundrel's trick; I shall conquer them, as I did Veii, in the Roman way, by courage, effort, weapons." He stripped the fellow, tied his hands behind his back, and gave him to the boys to drive back to Falerii, putting rods in their hands to scourge him as he went.

The reaction of the Faliscans was voluntary surrender:

"Senators, a victory which neither god nor men could begrudge, you and your general have won over us. We surrender to you because we believe (and what could be more handsome for a victor?) that life will be better under your administration than under our own laws."

Dignity and imperturbability (and their effect on lesser breeds) are illustrated by the deportment of the Roman gentry when the Gallic barbarians broke into the Forum (in 390 B.C.):

Clothed in the magnificent dress which those wear who drive the carriages of the gods at the games or celebrate triumphs, they sat in ivory chairs in the middle of their houses. . . .

With great reverence the Gauls gazed at the men sitting in the vestibules of their houses; and stood before them as if they were statues; in addition to their ornaments and dress, which were too splendid for mere mortals, they seemed very like gods in the majesty and dignity of their countenances. But when one of the Gauls stroked the long beard of Marcus Papirius (all beards were worn long in that day), Papirius struck him on the head with his ivory staff and enraged him. Papirius's death began the slaughter; the rest were cut down in their chairs.

When Pyrrhus was winning his Pyrrhic victories, his physician offered to poison him for the Romans: the Romans sent him back to Pyrrhus in chains. When Pyrrhus's emissary came to bribe the Roman general he found him cooking his own meal of turnips—and realized that a Roman could not be bribed. When Regulus was taken captive by the Carthaginians he was sent home on parole to persuade the Senate to make peace; he persuaded them to the contrary, and returned to Carthage to certain torture. Foreigners too recognized Roman probity and the Roman determination to fulfill engagements. Antiochus IV marched his army to within four miles of Alexandria and could surely have taken it. A Roman commissioner named Popilius Laenas, not an army, ordered him to desist, and when he temporized, "drew a circle around the king with the staff in his hand and said, 'Give me your answer before you step out of this circle.'" Antiochus departed out of Egypt. It is significant that when Symmachus wished to strengthen Roman patriotism (in the fourth century) his method of doing so was to multiply copies of Livy.

It was the special style of its public image which gave Rome its stability and which perpetuated the ideal in the fragments of the Empire after Rome itself fell. The style was given visible expression in monumental structures, large and solid and timeless, and in the majesty of its magistrates and the ritualistic pomp of its proceedings. All serious Latin literature is permeated with the ideal. Its effects are expressed in the deportment and responsibility of its governors and in the discipline of the governed. Needless to say, the ideal was not always realized, but it always remained the ideal. And as an ideal it shaped the public life of its successor states. That our own senior governing body is called a Senate, and that the seat of our Supreme Court is an obvious imitation of Roman public architecture, may be mere antiquarianism (it is more, for our founding fathers understood and sought to emulate the ancient pattern); what is more important is that the style of public life, the deportment of officials, the obligations of the governed, and the sense of duty to the state which informs the whole, are avatars of the Roman patterns.

A new polity formed by revolution could deal critically with antecedent tradition, and it was natural that a new republic should look to the classic example of republican organization in Rome. We clothe our president with high dignity, but we do not endow him with a charismatic mystique as ruling by divine right; what gave the theory authority and currency was the example of Rome and particularly the *Aeneid* of Vergil. The *Aeneid* did not have to be rediscovered at the Renaissance; all educated people knew it. Dante reveres Vergil as his guide, and echoes his ideas in his treatise *On Monarchy*. Rome was so fully accepted as part of the divine scheme that Brutus and Cassius, who betrayed a Caesar, are made to share the lowest part of the Inferno with Judas Iscariot, the betrayer of Christ.

The essential difference between the Roman theory and that of the disparate nationalisms which inherited it is that the Empire was virtually coextensive with the *oikoumene,* so that patriotism was not parochial, but rather loyalty to a world order. Greek political theory, and certainly Stoic, influenced Augustus's reorganization; the emperor was necessary as a director of the world order, but its minister rather than lord. The system soon turned into an iron autocracy, but so have other humane and liberal schemes of government. But when each of the later nationalities emulated Rome, there arose a diversity of patriotisms each claiming divine sanction and exclusive loyalty. The history of Thucydides deals with Greeks but in no sense promotes Greek nationalism as Livy's history of Rome purposefully does. Livy's nationalism is defensible because Rome's destiny was universal. The national histories of the countries of Europe were modeled not on Thucydides but on Livy. Again our histories are being liberated from national partisanships. The recognition of the importance of the individual regardless of the government he lives under is a return to humanism.

The fullest expression of the universality of Rome and one of its greatest contributions is in its majestic codes of law before which all men, regardless of place or race, stood equal. This too was an eventual product of the Hellenistic ferment and especially of Stoicism. The Greeks were extremely jealous of citizenship, for reasons mentioned above, and when the Athenians came into control of an empire they held absolute sway over it, as an Oriental monarch might have done. The theory of the equality of all men, adumbrated in the Greek enlightenment, became common currency in the Hellenistic Age. The *Pax Romana* or "Roman Peace" by which term the Romans referred to their dominion may have been a euphemism; "they make a solitude," the Briton said, "and they call it peace." But even discounting hypocrisy a mission of policing and civilizing the darker corners of the world is better than a stark claim to owning it. In its context the fine sentence *homo sum, humani nihil a me alienum puto* ("I am a man and nothing human is alien to me") is merely a justification of neighborly nosiness; but it describes one aspect of humanism which was peculiarly Roman. Perhaps it is a central aspect, for out of it other aspects of humanism grow.

Until the fifth century there were men who thought that the victory of Christianity must entail the ruin of humanist civilization. In 416, Rutilius Namatianus, who has been called the last poet of Rome, wrote a travel poem describ-

ing his sea journey home to his estates in Provence. While
waiting for sailing weather at Ostia, from which he could
see the Roman sky line, he wrote a moving apostrophe to
Rome:

> Queen of a world that you have made your home,
> amid the sky of stars, come hear me, Rome.
> Mother of manhood and of godhood, hear:
> within your shrines we feel the heavens near.
> You still we sing, we'll sing while fates permit.
> All men, alive, remember what you've done.
> Our hearts shall never cease to honour it
> till evil ruin blackens out the Sun.
>
> .   .   .   .
>
> You brought the nations one great fatherland,
> you raised the savage with your taming hand,
> broke him, but gave him laws to be his aid.
> A City of the scattered Earth you made.
>   (*Translated by* JACK LINDSAY)

But Christianity did not destroy Roman humanism.
Each was indeed affected by the other, and together they
achieved a kind of symbiosis to carry the culture of antiquity to the countries of Europe. With Christianity secure
even Christian poets could freely use traditional forms and
pagan imagery for even specifically Christian themes and
acknowledge the indebtedness of Christianity to the organization of the Roman Empire which prepared the way
for it. Prudentius (348–405), the best of the early Christian
poets, wrote a refutation of Symmachus's defense of the
statue of Victory twenty years before, but on grounds as
patriotic as Symmachus's own. Here is a portion:

Over all countries within the bounds of the western ocean,
over all lighted by Aurora's rosy dawning, raging Bellona had
confounded all things human and had armed savage hands to
inflict wounds one upon another. To bridle this madness God
taught the nations everywhere to bow their heads under the

same laws: all whom Rhine and Danube water, or gold-bearing Tagus, or great Ebro, all that Hesperian Tiber flows through or Ganges nourishes or the seven mouths of the warm Nile sustain—all these did God teach to be Romans. A shared law made them peers, intertwined them under a single name, brought the vanquished into the bonds of brotherhood. In regions most diverse life proceeds as if fellow-citizens of the same breed dwelt within the walls of a single ancestral city, as if all were at peace under their grandfathers' roof. Areas geographically remote, shores divided by the sea, now merge in allegiance to a single jurisdiction, now their trade and their handicrafts bring them to a single thronged market, now dwellers in disparate regions unite in solemn wedlock, and a single progeny is the issue of the mingled blood of diverse races. Such was the achievement of the enormous successes and triumphs of Roman power. It was for Christ, who was even then on his way, that the path was prepared; the general amity of our peace had long since paved it under the direction of Rome. . . . Now the earth is in concord: infuse it, Almighty, with thy presence; now, Christ, a world receives thee which peace and Rome hold together in a bond of union.

(Translated by M. J. THOMSON)

Prudentius feels no incongruity in naming pagan Aurora and pagan Bellona in a poem which concludes with a prayer to Christ.

CHAPTER 12
THE AVENUE OF SURVIVAL

What enabled the humanistic tradition to survive principalities and powers was its ability to lead an existence independent of them. When survival seemed to be threatened, first by dilution in the Hellenistic world and then by the overwhelming power of men of foreign speech, the separation between political suzerainty and the life of the spirit became conscious and purposeful. Hellenism became a kind of cult, which could command loyalty even under an alien power and which could even spread its evangel to alien people without incurring suspicion of subversiveness. If it had not done so classical culture would have been obliterated; because it did do so some men still study the classical languages and many men read classical books, and not merely for antiquarian interest.

The figure who best illustrates this phenomenon, and who may himself be in part responsible for making a particular body of knowledge and the outlooks and way of life it reflected into an independent and viable entity, is Plutarch, who lived in the late first century A.D. Of Plutarch as a paradigm of Hellenism we shall speak more fully in a moment, but first we must glance at his antecedents. As far back as we can reach Greek education had centered on literature; craftsmen must have had long and rigorous training in their special skills, as the superb workmanship and taste in their architecture and pottery and other crafts make abundantly plain. What we do hear about is their education in letters, for example, in this passage in Plato's *Protagoras* (325d):

> They send the boy to teachers, and enjoin them to see to his manners even more than to his reading and music; and the teachers do as they are desired. And when the boy has learned his letters and is beginning to understand what is written, as before he understood only what was spoken, they put into his hands the works of great poets, which he reads sitting on a bench at school; in these are contained many admonitions, and many tales, and praises, and encomia of ancient famous men, which he is required to learn by heart, in order that he may imitate or emulate them and desire to become like them. Then, again, the teachers of the lyre take similar care that their young disciple is temperate and gets into no mischief; and when they have taught him the use of the lyre, they introduce him to the poems of other excellent poets, who are the lyric poets; and these they set to music, and make their harmonies and rhythms quite familiar to the children's souls, in order that they may learn to be more gentle, and harmonious, and rhythmical, and so more fitted for speech and action; for the life of man in every part has need of harmony and rhythm.

Plato himself, curiously, shied away from the study of literature and banned Homer and good tragic poets (he would tolerate the bad) from his ideal Republic, not because he disliked literature—he was himself a very great literary artist—but because it might subvert the strict discipline he desiderated. Achilles is insubordinate to authority and uncontrolled in his passions. Plato's own Academy was devoted to philosophy and mathematics, which is to say it was specialist. In his autobiographical Seventh Epistle he says that his doctrine could not be acquired through books but only by long association of master and disciple. After sitting at Plato's feet for twenty years Aristotle diverged from his master, but his own Lyceum was even more specialist, being in effect a series of institutes for specialized study in various disciplines.

The School of Isocrates, which was roughly contemporary with the Academy, was neither exclusive nor specialist. Isocrates taught fine literary style and discoursed on politics. For these subjects students required knowledge of the past, and Isocrates seems to have been a pioneer in citing historical examples for their substance rather than as mere decoration. In other words, Isocrates was concerned, as Plato had not been, with perpetuating the qualities of Greekhood, and understood that the proper vehicle for the transmission of these qualities was their precipitate in Greek literature. Almost all the historians and orators of the fourth century of whom we know were disciples of Isocrates, not Plato. That perpetuation of Greekhood was his concern is shown by his advocacy of a crusade against the East in order to safeguard it, and that Greekhood rather than Greek blood was the paramount factor is shown by his statement that a non-Greek with Greek education is Greek.

One effect of Isocrates' educational program was that his library of classics came to constitute a virtual canon which all Greeks could be assumed to know. Authors and speakers in Christian centuries could assume familiarity with them and allude to them freely. Later writings may be recorded in scholarly books, but only the classics, centuries old, are cited in *belles lettres*. It was the program of Isocrates which has shaped European education to this day, which has kept humanism alive, and which has given Western civilization such unity as it possesses.

The first major crisis in the chain of survival was the Hellenistic Age, and here the role of the books is central. The first order of business in any new Greek settlement in the East was the establishment of a *gymnasion,* whose avowed aim was the perpetuation of Greekhood and whose main instrument was the Greek classics. In Alexandria the books were subject to a species of intense philological and critical study which was partly revived in the Renaissance and more fully emulated in the nineteenth century. About the first century, as has been noted above, literary education was so highly esteemed that it was thought to confer special privileges in a future existence. When as an adolescent in Syrian Samosata, Lucian was considering his future career, he was visited in a dream by two ladies, one representing the statuary's trade and the other *paideia* or liberal education. Here is Dame Culture's plea (*Enupnion* 10):

Be governed by me, and your first reward shall be a view of the many wondrous deeds and doings of the men of old; you shall hear their words and know them all, what manner of men they were; and your soul, which is your very self, I will adorn with many fair adornments, with self-mastery and justice and restraint and mildness, with consideration and understanding and fortitude, with love of what is beautiful, and yearning for what is great; these things it is that are the true and pure ornaments of the soul. Naught shall escape you either of ancient wisdom or of present avail; nay, the future too, with me to aid, you shall foresee; in a word, I will instil into you, and that in no long time, all knowledge human and divine.

(*Translated by* H. W. AND F. G. FOWLER)

Lucian's advocacy of *paideia* in this passage rests on the opulence and prestige which it brings to its possessors, and indeed these advantages continued to attach to *paideia*, especially in Byzantium but also, as we shall see, in Rome and its successors. Elsewhere, at least by implication, Lucian recommends true *paideia* as a prophylactic against corruption of taste and rationality. But aside from such practical considerations there were motives of piety, like those Isocrates' work suggests but more spiritual, which urged solicitous attention to the humanistic tradition. For this position our best example is in the life and works of Plutarch. Plutarch was born of a prominent family in Chaeronea in Boeotia, not far from Delphi, in the middle of the first century A.D. He was extremely learned and highly respected. Like other gifted Greeks he settled in Rome, and then despite the high professional and social success he achieved there he returned to his native place, and became market inspector of the provincial town of Chaeronea and priest of the obsolescent shrine at Delphi. The only explanation for the change that he gives is contained in a remark on the inadequacy of library facilities at Chaeronea: it is a small town indeed that he lives in, but if he moved away it would be even smaller.

But from his prolific works we may divine a more cogent reason. In Plutarch's eyes Greekhood took on the proportions of a cult and an evangel, and he devoted himself to its care and propagation. He lived in Greece because that was where the responsible heirs of Greekhood should be. He became a priest of Delphi because Delphi was the traditional hearth of Hellenism. He became market inspector because active participation in public life was the Greek way. He discoursed to the youth of his neighborhood on literature and philosophy and mathematics and music because these were essential parts of *paideia*. He wrote his *Parallel Lives* to show Greeks that Greek generals and statesmen had equaled or surpassed their Roman analogues; Greeks needed to be shown, for after more than two centuries of Roman domination they accepted Roman convictions of their own inferiority. He did not include poets and philosophers and artists because here the Romans themselves readily acknowledged Greek superiority. Greekhood is by no means limited to Greece, but other peoples are gauged according to their actual or potential participation in Greekhood. The religion of the Egyptians is not absurd, because it can be regarded as a special manifestation of Greek religion. The Romans are good because they do participate in Greekhood and foster it; an individual who fails markedly in this respect, like the Elder Cato, can be quite severely criticized. There is no slightest suggestion that Rome will one day fall or that Greece will one day recover its sovereignty. Greekhood is not being maintained as preparation for an irredentist movement, but for its own sake. Greekhood is not local but may one day embrace all mankind.

But even so prim a traditionalist as Plutarch can be independent in his views. He knows that Herodotus and Aristophanes are authentic classics, but he charges the one with malice against Boeotia and the other with crudities. His reverence for Plato is unbounded and his philosophy is Platonic at every step, and yet his essay on love, after following the *Symposium* as far as possible, concludes with an insistence on the superiority of conjugal over homosexual love. In other respects also, though he himself knows nothing of Christianity, Plutarch approaches Christian ethics. Words like *humanitarian, gentle, mild,* are frequent, there is a new reverence for womanhood and a new concern for the weak. The humanist tradition may be weakened in some respects but in others it is strengthened.

For us the great importance of Plutarch is that he is a prime vehicle and vessel of the humanist tradition. If he had not made Greekhood into a cult perhaps he would not have been so widely read and perhaps the heirs of Greekhood would be less numerous. In himself, Emerson and others to the contrary notwithstanding, Plutarch is of much lesser stature as artist or thinker than the authentic classics, but it was Plutarch whom Montaigne and Shakespeare used. Amyot's version of Plutarch, which Montaigne justly admired, itself became a French classic and enjoyed a very wide vogue. North's English version, which Shakespeare used, brought Plutarch to a wide English-reading public. Because he himself knew the whole range of the Greek experience and the Greek achievement at first hand and because his writings are so copious, Plutarch is the broadest channel to Europe of things Greek. But more important than the information he conveys is the attitude to it which he communicates. The disparate elements in the Greek tradition add up to a style which is the vehicle of civilization; for civilization to endure and flourish that style must be preserved and emulated.

The peoples of the East made themselves part of the Greek cultural stream by adapting their works to Greek modes and even translating their own classics, as the Old

Testament was translated, into Greek. The more stalwart Romans acquired a much larger proportion of the Greek cultural legacy by putting it into their own language. In every kind of cultural expression, in philosophy and art and in every department of literature, the Romans copied and adapted the work of the Greeks. It was natural that this should be so, for when the Romans reached the level of wealth and power to afford and appreciate the refinements of culture, the Greeks had already attained their apogee, and it would have been absurd to start a laborious ascent from the primitive when sophisticated masterpieces were available for exploitation. And not only did the Romans adopt the Greek achievement; they also adopted the reverent attitude to tradition which the Hellenistic world, in which they moved, had established.

Statuary, which is independent of language, could be imported without adaptation, and hundreds, perhaps thousands, of Greek statues were in fact brought to Italy. Sculpture produced in Rome, whether direct copies of Greek work or originals, was regularly the work of Greek craftsmen; even Lucian and Plutarch regard carving as an occupation not befitting a gentleman. Original Roman work, characteristically, consists mainly in realistic portraiture of Roman worthies or reliefs recording Roman prowess. Philosophy too was wholly Greek and taught by Greek teachers. Romans like Cicero or Seneca who wrote philosophic treatises (always practical rather than speculative) take pains to explain that they are laymen, not professional philosophers; even the craft of philosophy was unseemly for a Roman gentleman.

But the fullest vehicle for cultural transmission is of course literature, and Latin literature is inconceivable, often not wholly intelligible, without its Greek models. Its genres, its systems of versification, its mythology, are all Greek. It started with a direct translation from the Greek, made while the Greek translators of the Old Testament were still at work on the Septuagint. Because Livius Andronicus, a schoolmaster, had no adequate text to teach his

Roman pupils literature he made one by turning the *Odyssey* into Latin. The greatest Roman poet starts his career with *Eclogues,* that are sometimes little more than translations of Theocritus, continues with *Georgics,* in which he avows the inspiration of Hesiod, and crowns his work and Latin literature with the *Aeneid,* in which he is more independent and more masterful but which is still inconceivable without the models of *Iliad* and *Odyssey.* Horace, the outstanding lyric poet, bases his claim to originality and immortality on having been the first to introduce certain classical Greek measures into Latin poetry. Lucretius's great masterpiece leans heavily on Epicurean work. Both the comedies of Plautus and Terence and the tragedies of Seneca are frank adaptations of Greek plays. Cicero admits that his philosophical essays were "copies of the Greek to which I contribute only words, of which I have a great plenty." All cultured Romans knew Greek, and many went to Greece for higher education. Before the first century B.C. and after the first century A.D., they even wrote Greek. Roman historians who wrote in Greek (whose work is lost) represent the former group, and Marcus Aurelius is not alone in representing the latter. Even the closest Latin adaptations of Greek work have a characteristic Latin stamp, but even the most Roman of them carry on a large segment of the Greek tradition and, more important, Greek esteem for the tradition; and because European civilization was Latin rather than Greek, Rome is the keystone in the arch which springs from Hellas and descends to modern times.

Rome's provincial administration was efficient and vigorous and its subjects were generally content to discharge their obligations, but Romans never embarked on a purposeful program of cultural homogenization. They freely acknowledged that others might be better artists or astronomers or the like; their own mission was to insure peace and security so that these and other arts of civilization might flourish unhindered. This mission is put into words by the prophetic shade of Anchises, Aeneas's father, near the end of the sixth *Aeneid:*

> Others, well I know
> will forge the living bronze more gracefully,
> will from marble lifelike figures chase,
> plead causes better, and with pointer trace
> the journeyings of the heavens, and indicate
> the rising constellations: be thy thought,
> Roman, to hold the nations in your sway.
> These shall your arts be: terms of peace to name,
> to spare the vanquished and war down the proud.
>
> (*Translated by* E. DELABERE-MAY)

Rome was the world's policeman, not its teacher. In the eastern half of the Empire only the administration and army were Latin, otherwise Greek was the official as well as the vernacular language and Greek culture was little affected by Roman. But the West was more thoroughly and more permanently Romanized than the East had been Hellenized. The means were the same: willing emulation of Roman modes on the part of the natives, and schooling of the Roman type.

Initially Gauls and Spaniards and Britons resisted Rome, as might be expected, and a part of the resistance had a religious focus and inspiration in Druidism. That is doubtless the real reason why the Romans suppressed the Druids, but the Romans declared the suppression a police matter, to prevent human sacrifice. Their policy was not to interfere with local customs, yet in spite of this detachment, or perhaps because of it, the provincials chose to act like Romans. Upper-class natives lived in houses of the Roman type, dressed and dined in the Roman fashion, frequented Roman baths and Roman spectacles, were armed and drilled in the Roman manner, formed local political institutions, and carried on local political life like Romans and in buildings of Roman design, and, most important of all, received education of the Roman type and so came to accept the ideal image of Rome enshrined in Roman literature.

Gifted provincials might have the whole Empire for their arena. Several of Rome's best emperors came from Spain or Yugoslavia. Many of its greatest writers were men of provincial birth or extraction; Martial, Quintilian, and the Senecas were Spaniards. Their induction into Roman ways and the Roman outlook such men could acquire in local schools with Latin curricula. The schools of Gaul in particular came to surpass those of Rome itself. That is why the Romance languages, French and Spanish, Portuguese and Rumanian, are as transparently Latinate as Italian itself. In the long sweep of the history of humanism the destruction of Rome's political structure is only an incident. The cultural tradition and the style of Rome, which were themselves a continuation of the humanist tradition of the Greeks, marched forward and took root in lands the Greeks never knew.

The uncovering of classical texts which ushered in the humanist age was no such discovery as that of the ancient Cretan culture in our time, which exhibited a culture hitherto totally unknown, or even as that of the Babylonians or Hittites, which revealed the beginnings of a civilization of which we already knew the final products. The culture of the Middle Ages was not a rejection of the humanistic tradition, nor yet an acceptance of it like a windfall from a stranger, but a complete coalescence. As Roman Vergil is a different thing from Homer but still a vehicle for Homer's values and inconceivable without him, so is Christian literature of the Middle Ages different from antique Latin literature but inconceivable without it, and similarly a vehicle for ancient outlooks. Its premises, its metaphors, its numerous literary commonplaces (studied, for example, in Ernst Curtius's significantly named *European Literature of the Latin Middle Ages*), show that it is a living continuity, with no more alteration than is natural to a living organism. The flame of humanist culture did burn low in the so-

---

called dark centuries, especially in the tenth, but it was never wholly extinguished. Even in the dark tenth century, Hrotswitha, a nun of Gandersheim, wrote edifying plays in imitation of Terence; her *apologia* for doing so points to the path of Christian humanism:

There are some who cleave to the sacred pages but who, though they spurn other writings of the gentiles, read the fictions of Terence all too frequently, and in taking pleasure in the sweetness of his discourse are sullied by familiarity with wicked matters. Therefore I, the Strong Voice of Gandersheim, have not, while others cultivated him in perusal, refused to imitate him in utterance, to the end that by that same fashion of discourse by which the foul bawdiness of lewd women are set forth, the admirable chastity of holy virgins should be celebrated, according to the capacity of my small gifts.

CHAPTER 13
THE
INTEGRATED
CONTINUUM

Modern man is surrounded by echoes of antiquity, but all are not equally significant as manifestations of the humanistic tradition, and not all are equally recognizable. Indeed, those immediately recognizable are apt to be trivial; more important elements of the ancient legacy have been so thoroughly assimilated into the tradition of the race that they are no longer noticeable. We favor classical façades for monumental public buildings, we have many classical place names, we create new scientific terminology out of classical roots, we delight in classical mottoes on bottles and hatbands, and we call detergents and storage batteries by the names of ancient heroes. These are borrowings, like dress designs or coiffures copied from museum exhibits, and intended to be recognized as such. They are not evidence of the substantive operation of the tradition but only exploitations of it. They do prove that the classical tradition exists for otherwise it could not be exploited.

More meaningful is the continuing vogue of the ancient monuments, literary and other, in their original forms. Impressive physical remains not only in Athens and Rome but scattered over the Roman world from Scotland to the Euphrates bear mute witness to the glory that was Greece and the grandeur that was Rome. Increasing numbers visit the ancient sites and millions more have acquired familiarity with them through books and periodicals and television.

Good poets make fresh versions of ancient literature, producers present ancient drama, critics find new insights and interpretations of ancient thought. The most impressive remains of all, and the most important for maintaining the vitality of the tradition, are the ancient languages and literatures themselves, and there are many who study them, not as preparation for something else, but for their own sake.

Most important of all is the precipitate of humanism which has come down through the ages, extended or diminished or variously emphasized from generation to generation, but still in an unbroken stream. The lower reaches of the stream are by no means identical with its sources, as the Romance languages are not identical with Latin, but the changes have been natural growths and the deviations from the original unplanned. And the Romance languages have enriched others also; English is not a Romance language, but it would be utterly crippled if its Latin elements were removed. Architecture is a less significant vehicle than language, but may be a more tangible illustration of the same process. A cathedral is fully integrated into the culture of the age in which it was built and seems to be an original expression of that culture. In fact it is a straight-line development from the Roman basilica, from which it derives clerestory and apse, vestibule and interior colonnade. And so it is also with the intellectual and spiritual values which are of our own time but for which the ancient humanistic tradition has supplied the armature and suggested the contours.

For Westerners who seek to sort out the links in the chain of tradition it is natural to think first of the Latin heritage, which is indeed the easier to follow, but we must not forget that in the East Greek culture was transmitted in an uninterrupted stream, and without Rome as intermediary. In the early centuries of our era there were of course tensions between Christians and pagans, but far less acrimonious than those in Rome, because Christian teachers in the East—Clement and Origen in the second century, Basil and Gregory and John Chrysostom in the fourth, to name outstanding examples—were usually men who had received a thorough Greek education and themselves promoted it. How normal it was for Christians to study the pagan classics is shown by their reaction to the prohibition against their use in Christian schools decreed by Julian called the Apostate (332–363). A father and son, both called Apollinaris, made a new Homer for school use out of the Pentateuch and a Plato out of the Gospels. Though Julian's revival of paganism was short-lived, his encouragement of ancient learning was more effective. Here is part of a panegyric addressed to him in January 362:

You, mightiest of emperors, you, I say, have restored to their dignity the virtues which had been exiled and discredited; you have kindled the flame of study which had been quenched; philosophy, which had been suspect and not only stripped of its honors but reprobated and indicted, you not only freed from prosecution but clothed in purple and bound on her head gold and gems and seated on a royal throne. But a little before we had fixed our timid gaze upon earth after the fashion of lowly quadrupeds; now we can look up to the sky and contemplate the stars with fearless eyes.

Julian's was the last reaction against Christianity; after him there was no occasion for truculence on either side, and the two cultures entered into a peaceful blend. A figure who well represents the blend is Synesius of Cyrene (ca. 370–412). Synesius was a country squire, fought brigands and hunted, dabbled in Neoplatonic philosophy, prided himself on his descent from the Heraclides of Sparta, and nevertheless became a faithful bishop of Ptolemais in North Africa and wrote fine Christian hymns in Doric dialect and ancient meters. It is a new thing for a master of such a form to devote it to Christian hymns, and a new thing for a believing Christian to be willing to use a form with such pronounced pagan associations. In such a poem

as the following, where the Child of the Virgin of Solyma
descends to Tartarus and Hades and Cerberus, Christianity
and Hellenism have become one flesh:

Beloved, glorious, blest,
Seed of the Virgin of Solyma,
Thy praise I sing,
Who didst from the garden of Thy Father drive
The fount of guile,
The mighty serpent of earth,
Which gave the offspring of that earliest birth
The fruit abjured, the nurse that made death thrive.

Thine, O Father, diademed and glorious,
Child of the Virgin of Solyma,
Thy praise I sing.

Thou didst descend even unto the earth,
And, clad in semblance mortal,
Didst dwell with us,
The creatures of a day,
A little while;
Thou didst descend below the lowest portal
Of Tartarus,
Where Death
The myriad hosts of spirits shepherdeth.

Upon that day
Ancient Hades, child of Eld,
Shuddered when he beheld
Thy face, and Cerberus,
The folk-devouring hound,
From Hell's threshold slunk away.

Then didst Thou from their pain
Wherein they bound
So long had lain
The souls of all Thy holy ones redeeming,
Lead them in mystic revel without stain,
Dancing to their Father's house again.

Thee, O Father, diademed and glorious,
Child of the Virgin of Solyma.
Thee I sing.

. . . .

(*Translated by* L. P. CHAMBERLAYNE)

In the eastern half of the Empire the Byzantines were even more solicitous than the Romans of their linguistic and literary legacy. That is why professors of classical Greek were available to Italy after the fall of Constantinople, and that is why modern Greek is less removed from ancient than Italian is from Latin. The Arabic and then Turkish invasions deprived Byzantium of its dominions in Asia, and the Asiatic peoples reverted to their vernaculars, now, however, with a considerable admixture of Greek words. But meanwhile Byzantium had carried its culture to the Slavic countries in the North. It was from Constantinople that Saints Cyril and Methodius Christianized the Slavic lands of eastern Europe in the ninth century, and as is the way of missionaries they carried a full load of Byzantine culture along with their Christianity. That is why the Slavic countries are still Orthodox, that is why the Cyrillic script, used in Russia and Bulgaria, is rather like Greek than Latin, and that is why even proletarian Russia carries on lively study of Greek antiquity.

Byzantium also affected the West directly, not through the mediation of Rome, through the career of Charlemagne (742–814). Through his emissaries Charlemagne was in close touch with Byzantium, and it was from Byzantium that he adopted his revolutionary and highly efficient machinery of administration and the etiquette and dress appropriate to an imperial court, and it was in part by Byzantine example that he initiated the revival of learning we call Carolingian. And it was partly in opposition to the theoretical claim of the Eastern emperors to suzerainty over the whole Empire which the emperors of antiquity (whose legitimate successors they were) had ruled that Charlemagne set up the theory of his own Holy Roman Empire. The crusaders who passed through Constantinople may have brought some Greek influence back with them, but they did little to promote the cause of letters. In the fires and rapine that attended the sack of Constantinople by the Crusaders of the Fourth Crusade in 1204, Greek literature suffered a much greater loss than it had suffered at the burning of the Alexandrian Library nearly a millennium before. "The literature of the Greeks," as Gibbon observes at the end of his sixtieth chapter, "had almost centered in the metropolis: and without computing the extent of our loss, we may drop a tear over the libraries that have perished in the triple fire of Constantinople." The channel to Europe via the eastern Rome is nevertheless broader than is sometimes assumed. In the fifteenth century, when Constantinople fell, it was still able to transmit the Greek legacy and Italy was now prepared to receive it and join it to its own broad and direct channel to northern Europe.

A more immediate and direct channel to Europe for the organism which was Rome was the organism of the Catholic Church. Constantine's conversion to Christianity is ascribed by the Church historian Eusebius to his vision of the *labarum* bearing the legend IN HOC SIGNO VINCES at the Battle of the Milvian Bridge, but secular historians have doubted the story and ascribed Constantine's toleration to practical political considerations. The administrative structure of the Empire had become much weakened, and the organization of the Church had become correspondingly more efficient, with bishops exercising more authority and enforcing greater discipline than provincial administrators were able to secure. The Church, then, would be an adjunct to the state in procuring order and discipline in the Empire. Whether or not such an interpretation is acceptable it was natural for the organism of the Church to make use of an existing model. With Latin as its universal language, with regional dioceses corresponding to late imperial divisions, with disciplined obedience to the majestic structure, and with a hierarchy corresponding to the Roman "course of honors," the parallels to Rome are striking. "Catholic" means universal, and the unity of Europe which the Church fostered was a conscious continuation of the unity of Europe which Rome had welded together. In a later age a man like Erasmus who agreed with Luther's condemnation of current abuses in the Church and who seemed ready to join Luther's movement refrained from doing so because the Church was a visible cement of Europeanism which he did not wish to see fragmented by regional secessions. Erasmus's advocacy of the use of Latin as a vernacular is another indication of his European rather than national loyalty.

Just as Rome and its dominions, after initial hostility, achieved symbiosis and a readiness to acknowledge one another's beneficent role, so it was with Rome and Christianity also. Before the symbiosis there had been bloody persecutions, and even after Constantine's edict made Christianity lawful there were nostalgic traditionalists, like Symmachus, who deplored the subversion of the venerable ideal of Rome which had produced and safeguarded civilization and pointed to the fall of Rome as retribution for the neglect of tradition. The charge was refuted by St. Augustine in *The City of God* and by his pupil Orosius in his *Seven Books Against the Pagans:* history showed that the pagan deities had never been able to avert disasters, and so far from causing the fall, Christianity had alleviated its effects.

While the partisans of the Roman tradition were still restive Christians were accepting so much of that tradition as was not offensive to them as an adjunct of Christianity. Prudentius, whose poem has been cited above, was not merely a poet who was Christian but a Christian poet. It is more significant of symbiosis that poets who were faithful Christians would write in the pagan manner as if they were oblivious of Christianity. The great bulk of the work of Ausonius follows the main literary tradition, including the usual imagery and apparatus of gods; when he shows his Christianity it is as if he put on a Sunday suit to go to church. Claudius Claudianus (ca. 370–405), a generation later than Ausonius, makes even fuller use of the pagan tradition in his very prolific works and is even less obviously a Christian. Even in his epithalamium on the Christian marriage of the Emperor Honorius to Stilichos's daughter Maria there is no mention of Christian usages; Juno is still the patroness of marriage. Reconciliation of the cultural values of Rome with professed Christianity and churchly preferment is best illustrated by Sidonius Apollinaris, the chief literary figure of the fifth century, who could be bishop of Clermont and call Rome (in one of his letters which consciously emulated Cicero's and Pliny's) "domicile of law, school of literature, senate house of merit, apex of the universe, fatherland of liberty, sole polity of the whole world." About the year 400 Macrobius, whose *Saturnalia* centers on literary tradition, writes, "antiquity we must always venerate if we are wise."

The sixth century begins what has usually been called the Dark Ages, and it may be significant that Pope Gregory (540–604), whose achievements as churchman and statesman entitle him to the appellation "the Great," could hold that "The praises of Christ cannot be pronounced by the same lips as the praises of Jove" and "It is altogether inappropriate to keep the language of the Divine Oracles in subjection to the rules of [the grammarian] Donatus." Contemporary Latin writings do show marked deviations from classical usages in grammar. In the *History of the Franks* of Gregory of Tours (538–594) the refinements of syntactical subordination are blurred and prepositions sometimes replace case endings. But even if Latin lost its classical purity there was never a thought of abandoning it, and even in the hands of men who were indifferent to ancient tradition it communicated that tradition nevertheless.

But even through the Dark Ages, and especially in the Carolingian revival, the tradition of a purer Latinity and less inhibited scholarship flourished, not only in Continental centers but also in England. The *Historia ecclesiastica gentis Anglorum* of the Venerable Bede (673–735) shows ample knowledge. A pupil of Bede was Egbert, Archbishop of York, and Egbert's pupil Alcuin (735–804) was the most learned and influential scholar of his age. As head of the School at York, Alcuin made its library the best of any in England or France. From 782 to 790 he was head of the school attached to the court of Charlemagne, and thus was responsible for the systematization of learning and of book production in Charlemagne's age. John of Salisbury, (1110–1180), insisted (like his younger and better-known contemporary Abelard) on the importance of secular literature as an indispensable aid to sacred studies. Two of his younger contemporaries in England show expert knowledge of secular tradition. The Welshman Giraldus Cambrensis (1147–1222) wrote, among many other things, a history of the conquest of Ireland, and Walter Map, Archdeacon of Oxford in 1196, wrote Latin versions of the legends of Lancelot of the Lake, The Quest of the Holy Grail, and the Death of Arthur.

These few out of the more numerous names that might be cited show that the tradition was continually vital from antiquity onward, that it was not a preserve for isolated scholars in their studies but touched the wider world of literate men, and that it became a fusion not only of ancient and Christian matter but of local vernacular traditions also. The revival of learning, which we shall glance at in the chapter following, was by no means a new discovery across a gulf of centuries nor even a sudden awakening from a comatose state, but only a new kind of emphasis. The vernacular writers whom we shall examine are truer evidence of the continuing vitality of the humanistic tradition than the self-conscious Latin writings which were calculated to illustrate the continuity of the ancient forms. Even euphuism can have its uses, as is shown by the example of the Second Sophistic in the second century B.C., but it can very easily fall into absurdity, as can be illustrated by the debate on Ciceronianism in the Cinquecento. Under the leadership of Cardinal Pietro Bembo, who was papal secretary to Leo X, a society of *literati* bound its members by oath not to use any word which could not be found in

Cicero. Into the Latin of the Church Bembo introduced such terms as *res publica* for the Church and *magistri* for its officials. His dating is by Kalends, Nones, and Ides. He calls nuns *virgines vestales,* the saints *divi,* the cardinals *senatores.* The Virgin Mary is *dea ipsa;* he is unable to mention the Holy Ghost. The issue of "Ciceronianism" aroused a great tempest between those who favored Bembo's position and those who opposed it; chief among the latter was Erasmus, the truest humanist of all. It was impossible for the Ciceronians to prevail, for the Latin tradition was too deeply rooted and there were too many things in the world for which Cicero could supply no vocabulary. If they had prevailed Latin would have been doomed at once as a medium for communication. If the language of Cicero had retained the elasticity and viability which Erasmus for one tried to give it perhaps Europe might have been better able to achieve the ecumenical ideal of Rome. But if the ancient languages were the prime vehicles of the humanistic tradition they were by no means the sole, nor, one is tempted to add, the most efficient instruments for giving it expression in a changed world. It is humanism rather than its linguistic medium which is the cohesive element that provides a basis for pan-Europeanism.

CHAPTER 14

THE
HUMANIST
AGE

The revolution of the Hellenistic Age which the humanist tradition proved able to survive was political and social in character, only to a slight degree scientific and technological. But the revolution which the humanist tradition must now confront is mainly scientific and technological; we must therefore turn to a historical conjuncture which was like the Hellenistic Age in enlarging men's outlooks but in which science and technology played a leading role. Such a conjuncture is the age we call humanist. The revolution introduced by the invention of firearms and of printing, by the discovery of the properties of the magnet and of heliocentric astronomy, is of the same order as that introduced by the technological improvements vouchsafed man in the myth of Prometheus, or like the revolution which confronts us today. A work like the *Divine Comedy* is as far from the primitive as anything man has produced, but it belongs before the Renaissance and is inconceivable after it except as a tour de force. What makes it inconceivable is not the rediscovery of ancient books—Dante himself had read enough of them—but the new scientific outlooks, of which the revived interest in antiquity was rather a consequence than a cause. But if the classics did not provide the initial impulse for the new outlooks they did give them shape and substance and effected not only a survival but a flowering of the humanist tradition.

The salient difference between the waning Middle Ages and the burgeoning Renaissance is not in the quantity of Latin that was read but in the quality of the general temper; a gray and gloomy twilight gives way to a bright and cheerful dawn. In his learned and perceptive *The Waning of the Middle Ages* Huizinga writes:

At the close of the Middle Ages, a sombre melancholy weighs on people's souls. Whether we read a chronicle, a poem, a sermon, a legal document even, the same impression of immense sadness is produced by them all. It would sometime seem as if this period had been particularly unhappy, as if it had left behind only the memory of violence, of covetousness and mortal hatred, as if it had known no other enjoyment but that of intemperance, of pride and cruelty.

Now as in the Hellenistic Age the new concern with individual man dispersed the weight of the environment. The dominant and significant direction of the new outlooks was towards heightened importance of the individual. Here is the new conception of man, as proclaimed by Pico della Mirandola:

Then the Supreme Maker decreed that unto Man, on whom He could bestow nought singular, should belong in common whatsoever had been given to his other creatures. Therefore he took man, made in his own individual image, and having placed him in the center of the world, spake to him thus: "Neither a fixed abode, nor a form in thine own likeness, nor any gift peculiar to thyself alone, have we given thee, O Adam, in order that what abode, what likeness, what gifts thou shalt choose, may be thine to have and to possess. The nature allotted to all other creatures, within laws appointed by ourselves, restrains them. Thou, restrained by no narrow bounds, according to thy own free will, in whose power I have placed thee, shalt define thy nature for thyself. I have set thee midmost the world, that thence thou mightest the more conveniently survey whatsoever is in the world. Nor have we made thee either heavenly or earthly, mortal or immortal, to the end that thou, being, as it were, thy own free maker and molder, shouldst fashion thyself in what form may like thee best. Thou shalt have power to decline unto the lower or brute creatures. Thou shalt have power to be reborn unto the higher, or divine, according to the sentence of thy intellect." Thus to Man, at his birth, the Father gave seeds of all variety and germs of every form of life.

(Translated by J. A. SYMONDS)

As man shook off his gloom and moved into the center of the world his attitude towards it changed. Man's view of himself moved from the idealistic to the realistic, a utilitarian sanction for conduct took the place of a transcendental, a scientific rationalization of reality of a religious. Attitudes to external authority became more critical; its claims were subjected to the test of reason, and glorification of faith gave way to a suspicion of its validity. The shift from otherworldliness to a livelier concern with life in this world served to discredit asceticism and produced a bias in favor of pleasure instead of against it. Even in theology there was a heightened concern for the salvation of the individual. These new directions are all accepted premises in the ancient humanistic tradition, which could therefore supply inspiration and forms of expression. It was inevitable that the experience of the past should be emulated and receive new growth.

A tangible expression of the enhanced importance of man is style, and the most obvious characteristic of the Renaissance is a new attention to style. Sometimes this was expressed in a literal transcription of ancient modes, as in the rather ludicrous career of Cola di Rienzi (1313–1354) who donned a toga and proclaimed himself tribune in order to reinstitute the polity of the ancient republic; eventually Cola's program turned into a primitive fascism and he himself came to a bad end. But the toga and ancient title and program did not strike intelligent contemporaries as ludicrous. A notable style was a thing to be welcomed. In literary style the authority of classical tradition was even more exigent than it had been in later antiquity; the achievement for which the earliest humanists are properly known is their new appreciation of ancient forms and their emulation of them. It was the vehicle of form, as has been observed above, that attracted and gave shape to new content.

If style is an expression of the individual it follows that the individual wishes his identity to be known. Among the Greeks ambition for personal recognition amounted to an obsession, and a convenient if superficial index of the resumption of ancient norms is the importance again attached to names and signatures. In Homer men are motivated by a drive towards distinction and the renown which distinction brings, and this Homeric ethic informed all of Greek life. "May I have neither gold in my house nor skill to sing a sweeter song than Orpheus if my fortune is to be hid from the eyes of men," says Jason in Euripides' *Medea*, but the sentiment is a commonplace. Poets and artists and politicians have their names recorded, potters sign their work. Everyone knew the names of the architects who designed the Parthenon and of the sculptor who decorated it. Anonymity entered from the East, where the institution is enormously greater than the individual and service to it the individual's complete fulfillment. Most of the books in Scripture and its peripheries are anonymous or even pseudepigraphic, that is to say, they bear the name of some great personage, David or Solomon or Enoch, who cannot have written them, in order to obtain greater credit. Of the two books of the Maccabees in the Apocrypha the first, which is a translation of a Semitic original, is anonymous, and the second, which is an epitome of a Greek original, bears the name of its author, Jason of Cyrene. In Rome too the institution transcended the man: where Achilles is obsessed with self, Aeneas is the disciplined servant of a cause. Roman literary figures consciously strive for immortality because they are heirs of the Greek literary tradition. But except in literature fewer and fewer names are recorded.

After the revival men are as eager to record their names as they had been in classical Greece. Artists sign their works and otherwise emphasize their identity. Their individualities are recorded in biographies like Vasari's or even in an autobiography like Cellini's; biography of such a sort had not been written since Plutarch. The very title of such a work as Pico della Mirandola's *On the Dignity of Man* is significant.

In literary criticism, whose function is to safeguard canons of style, we should expect that the ancient tradition would be scrupulously guarded, and so in fact it was. Casual utterances of the ancients, or misunderstandings of them (as in the alleged three dramatic unities of Aristotle) were exaggerated into inexorable laws. But the dicta of the critics only defined and prescribed acceptable style; they did not obviate new content. The *Art of Poetry* of Jerome Vida (1490–1566), which was enthusiastically admired by John Milton and Alexander Pope, can really be summarized in a single sentence: to write good poetry you must emulate Vergil with the greatest conscientiousness. In his own *Christiads* Vida does indeed scrupulously follow Vergilian forms and language, but his outlook (to say nothing of his subject) is wholly new. After Vida even criticism, though it still depended on the ancients, became more independent. The *Poetics* of Julius Caesar Scaliger (the name is significant) in seven books and 944 pages (1561) is longer than all the ancient critics taken together, and prides itself on its originality. "The Greeks are mistaken," writes Scaliger, "if they think we have taken anything from them except to improve it."

The influence of ancient literary theory upon the literature of the humanist age, first in Latin and then in the vernaculars, is palpable. It is most palpable in the more spacious forms upon which the ancients themselves bestowed a high degree of stylization, especially in drama and epic. Drama was cultivated because the ancient examples showed that it was a dignified and highly artistic enterprise, not a pastime for carnival mobs. Early efforts, in Latin and then the vernacular, were little more than imitations, sometimes unperceptive, of classical originals. But even plays which adhered strictly to ancient forms and were written in Latin could be permeated by and propagate the new outlooks. George Buchanan (1506–1582), the Scottish humanist, who was a boyhood teacher of Montaigne, translated the *Alcestis* and the *Medea* of Euripides, and wrote original plays entitled *Jephthah's Daughter* and *John the Baptist*. The choice of the first two out of the whole corpus of tragedy shows that he appreciated their value as arguments against conventional degradation of women and foreigners; the latter two are outspoken assertions of the worth of the individual, and oppose authoritarianism in government and religion which overrides individual choice. Even in towering creative spirits like Shakespeare the use of poetry and lofty rhetoric, to say nothing of occasional themes, follows the example of ancient drama. In playwrights like Molière and Racine not only forms and themes but sometimes long stretches of content are adapted from the ancients.

Epic was cultivated because the ancients had held that the composition of an epic poem was the noblest achievement mortality could aspire to. There is little other reason for Boccaccio to have undertaken his *Teseide* or Petrarch his Latin *Africa*. All, like Vida's *Christiads* mentioned above, premise complete familiarity with the *Aeneid* for their proper comprehension. The *Lusiads* of the Portuguese Camoëns (1524–1580), which is a much greater and more original and deeply felt poem, plays a constant counterpoint to the *Aeneid* in design and detail. The example of ancient epic is less obvious in the *Jerusalem Delivered* of Tasso (1544–1595) and much less in the *Orlando Furioso* of Ariosto (1474–1533) and in his predecessors Boiardo and Pulci; but the enterprise of writing long narrative poems is still derived from the ancient example.

The culmination of humanist epic, and of course the

most familiar example of the genre for English readers, is *Paradise Lost*. Milton does indeed stand outside his age; it is hard to think of him in the moral atmosphere of the Restoration or the intellectual atmosphere of Descartes and Spinoza, who belong to his century. But perhaps his timelessness shows the viability of the tradition, which Milton openly acknowledges. He deliberately classes his poem with Homer's and Vergil's. When he comes to describe the Fall of man at the beginning of the ninth book he says:

> Sad task, yet argument
> Not less but more Heroic than the wrauth
> of stern *Achilles* on his Foe pursu'd
> Thrice Fugitive about *Troy* Wall; or rage
> Of *Turnus* for *Lavinia* disespous'd,
> Or *Neptun's* ire or *Juno's,* that so long
> Perplex'd the *Greek* and *Cytherea's* son.

Milton's first line declares his subject, like Homer's and Vergil's, and he invokes the Muse, not of Helicon, this time, but of Oreb or Sinai, and for a flight that will soar above the Aonian (Homeric) mount. Epithets and similes are in the ancient style, the books number twelve, and the heavily Latinate vocabulary and word order and syntax are almost a travesty of the normal English he uses elsewhere. But for all its fidelity to ancient form and for all its piety there are touches (aside from the artillery) even in *Paradise Lost* (to say nothing of Milton's prose writings) which reveal the effects of the new humanism. Why, in the first place, should the ways of God to man need to be justified at all? And why should Satan, in the early parts of the poem, be so admirably self-sufficient? But the form is significant in itself. Remarkable as it may be that a great poet should choose so classicizing a style for the work he proposed as his masterpiece, it is more remarkable that his audience was so steeped in classical style as to appreciate and applaud his work.

If Milton exemplifies the survival of ancient literary

style, Descartes and Spinoza exemplify more fully the revival of intellectual style. For the first time since the end of antiquity the law of contradiction obtains. No longer does the philosopher accept a body of doctrine as an unquestioned datum and then accommodate his own speculations to its premises; rather he starts with a clean slate, as the Ionian philosophers and their successors had done, and pursues truth by uninhibited reason. That is why Spinoza proceeds by a geometric method, and he uses Latin because it is a closer approach to mathematical symbols than vernacular language. His intellectual style, far more important than literary style, is like the Greek. He sees things *sub specie aeternitatis,* as the Greeks had done; he equates God and nature (*deus sive natura*) as the Stoics had done. God's incapacity to perform miracles (being synonymous with nature he cannot go counter to it) and his detachment from human concerns ("teleology is the last refuge of fools") suggest the Greek notion of disparate spheres for men and gods. If the Greeks had wished men to love God they would have described that love, as Spinoza does, as "intellectual." His aim Spinoza states as follows:

Sedulo curavi humanas actiones non ridere, non lugere, neque detestari, sed intellegere.

I have been at great pains not to laugh at human actions, nor to grieve over them, nor to abominate them, but to understand them.

No more than the philosophy of the Greeks has Spinoza's philosophy or his program become an orthodoxy; but after him men have learned to think of philosophy and examine philosophical doctrines, including those of the Greeks, differently. The dialogue which the Greeks initiated was continued in the Greek mode. And philosophy again began to touch the lives of man. The *philosophes* who prepared the way for the French revolution were steeped in philosophy and several were particularly attracted by Stoicism, and it may be that Stoic teachings of human equality had something to do with spreading the doctrine in the modern world.

At a more accessible level and more directly effective in communicating significant strands of the ancient tradition are the thoughtful writers, mainly in prose, whose work is classed as *belles lettres*. Petrarch and Boccaccio and the other pioneers of the Renaissance deserve their fame for having awakened men to the attractions of the tradition, but their own original works are mere *belles lettres* and are little read. But in the work of the authors of the fifteenth and sixteenth century which have a sure place not only in histories of literature but in the reading of bookish people the world over it is remarkable that the peculiar quality of each rests upon and propagates outlooks which belong to the ancient tradition. We must see how that tradition informs the writings of this group, and first in the work of Machiavelli, who is first in time.

In an important sense Machiavelli is more classical than Livy, because he is more unsentimental and more universal. In his perspicacious essay *On How History Should Be Written* Lucian said (41):

There stands my model then: fearless, incorruptible, independent, a believer in frankness and veracity; one that will call a spade a spade, make no concession to likes and dislikes, nor spare any man for pity or respect or propriety; an impartial judge, kind to all, but too kind to none; a literary cosmopolite with neither suzerain nor king, never heeding what this or that man may think, but setting down the thing that befell. . . . The historian's position should be precisely that of Zeus in Homer, surveying now the Mysians', now the Thracian horsemen's land.

That is how Thucydides had written his history; though he himself had been general on one side in the Peloponnesian War he deals with, he is equally fair to the other side. What he is interested in is the universal principles applicable to men in war, and when he enumerates the motives for war he makes fear and interest more important than honor. And so Polybius had written his Greek history of Rome; if he is less elegant than Thucydides he is even more pragmatic, to use his own favorite description of his work. His pragmatic view of the utility of Roman religion, for example, has been cited in an earlier chapter. Machiavelli knew and used Polybius, but when he says that it is good for a ruler to favor religion but not necessarily to be religious, he is severely criticized.

In his *Discourses on the First Ten Books of Livy* Machiavelli neither glorifies Rome nor indulges in moral homilies, but analyzes policies and leaders from the point of view of their efficacy in maintaining the structure of the state and shows the rationale of political success or failure. The better-known *Prince* is a similar guide for maintaining the stability of government by a prince. Given the subject, the treatment is reasonable, for to maintain his power a ruler must indeed be devious and ruthless. Tyrants like Hitler and Mussolini may have learned their tactics from Machiavelli, but in fact all rulers, those before Machiavelli as well as those after, have had to be Machiavellian. If Machiavelli is passionate in his exposition it is the passion of a researcher; as the last chapter of the *Prince* shows, he was a devoted Italian patriot and his own ideal was a unified Italy. He is called diabolic because, following the Greeks, he looked at the essential nature of man, not at the trappings with which convention had clothed him. He is an important channel for conveying the humanistic tradition to the modern world.

Erasmus, who shared Machiavelli's birth year and outlived him, is not nearly so controversial a figure. His interest was not in politics but in scholarship in the original sense, and he wrote in Latin, but no man has ever enjoyed greater popular renown and esteem for his bookishness. In his case there can be no doubt that he was a conscious continuator of the ancient tradition, and he did more than any man to propagate that tradition. The numerous scholarly editions of texts by which he made ancient authors accessible to the scholarly world have been improved upon and are important only in the history of scholarship. But of his nontechnical work, some—like the *Adagia,* which is simply a collection of quotable nuggets out of ancient literature—went through at least sixteen printings and broadcast some knowledge of the outlooks and the actual words of the ancients far and wide. Classical tags in the writings of men who knew the classics at first hand often came from the *Adagia* and even follow the order in which they appear there. The *Praise of Folly* satirizes superstition and similar deviations from rationality with humanistic sanity and urbanity. A similar temper characterizes the *Colloquies,* which are the most attractive of Erasmus's writings for the modern reader. Selections from the *Colloquies,* especially those prepared by convinced Protestants, always contain the satirical pieces on superstitious pilgrimages, unspiritual mendicants, ignorant or venal clergy, the unnatural discipline of nunneries; and the introductions to such selections suggest that such criticism is the principal object of the *Colloquies.* Actually these pieces occupy no more than their proper share of attention in a range which includes government, social and domestic questions, vignettes of ordinary life with ordinary casts of characters, sketches and short stories. So far from being hostile to religion they show how piety can be combined with learning, art, urbanity, and pleasant living; in a word, they communicate the humanist ideal. This lesson, whose implications are profounder than they initially seem, is really the burden of Erasmus's thought, and it becomes clearer with the increments the book received from edition to edition. The initial aim was a textbook for speaking Latin, and at least a collateral object of the expanded work was to demonstrate that pure Latin could be used as a vernacular for all the concerns and encounters of life. The book starts, as phrase books for foreign languages usually do, with formulas for ordinary greetings and polite exchanges. These become richer and more complicated as new situations and expressions for dealing with them are introduced, until the pieces turn into complete stories. In such a piece as that called "The Godly Feast" the conversation includes discussions of weather, vegetation, works of art, food and drink and other tangibles, as well as books and manners and ideas. Erasmus's promotion of Latin as an international vernacular, his consistent opposition to war, his unwillingness to participate in the Reformation, all suggest an ecumenical ideal of Europeanism to carry the ancient humanist tradition forward. The ideal of a cultural *oikoumene* had been put forward by the Greeks and enlarged and systematized by the Romans; the humanists, and Erasmus in particular, refurbished the old design and gave it new vigor.

All of the men in the group we are dealing with were faithful sons of the Church, but only Thomas More (1478–1535) carried his loyalty so far as to suffer martyrdom for it; four hundred years later he was made a saint of the Church. It is therefore a sign of humanistic tolerance that persecution for deviation from orthodoxy is forbidden in More's *Utopia*. Indeed the structure of society in *Utopia* is wholly subversive of the established order. The first book of *Utopia* is a sharp attack upon the institution of private property, which must necessarily negate the rights of the individual based on human equality, and the second prescribes the structure of a society in which gradations due to possessions are eliminated. Houses must be exchanged periodically, and clothing is all of the same color and quality. Meals are taken in common, but if an individual chooses to eat poorly prepared food alone rather than good food in public he may do so. Magistracies are careers open to talent; they carry dignity but no other emolument. If the authoritarianism necessary to enforce this discipline is necessarily strict, it is only a police measure to prevent exploitation of the weak by the strong and to ensure the maximum of leisure for all; facilities for study and other intellectual pursuits are provided. But no one is forced to study or listen to lectures. The system is not so utopian that all men are expected to have equal intellectual endowments as well as civic rights. Work like the butcher's or soldier's is relegated to the insensitive, not as degradation but because such occupations degrade the sensitive. Romance and chivalry are destroyed at a sweep. Young people intending to marry are required to see one another nude beforehand, of course with a proper chaperone: would a man buy a horse without removing its saddle? In case of war a graded tariff for the assassination or defection of enemy officers is advertised, with the result that many come over of their own accord to collect the reward.

There can be no doubt that the direct inspiration for *Utopia* comes from the Greeks; early in their history the Utopians had received and mastered a shipment of Greek books—except for passages damaged in transit. The obvious model is the *Republic* of Plato, but there were many Greek speculations on the ideal state both before and after Plato which More knew of. The common meals to which the whole populace is entitled certainly come from Herodotus's utopian description of the long-lived Ethiopians (3.18 ff.): "The table of the sun . . . is a meadow in the skirts of the city full of the boiled flesh of all manner of beasts, which the magistrates are careful to store with meat every night, and whosoever likes may come and eat during the day." The Ethiopians disdain dyed garments as deceitful and degrade gold by applying it to menial uses for which it is inferior to iron. There are traces of several utopias located on imaginary islands written in the Hellenistic Age. Euhemerus's showed that the Olympians were mortals who had been deified for services to mankind, and Iambulus's was a vehicle for Stoic doctrine. Lucian's *True History* starts as a parody of the latter and itself turns into a kind of utopia. More's *Utopia* is then a continuation of an ancient tradition revised in the spirit of the new humanism.

Utopian fiction has an advantage over direct criticism of the existing order and specific injunctions for reforming it because it clothes its novel ideas in flesh and blood and shows them in operation; the inadequacies of the old are sufficiently exposed by the superiority of the new. In the humanist age others besides More used analogous fictions to criticize the old and suggest the new; in Rabelais (1494–1553), whose learning is as prodigious as his ebullience, there are several visits to imaginary places where the old is tacitly ridiculed and improvements suggested. But in none, and in no other author, is the ancient tradition so obvious as in the fanciful Abbey of Thélème (*Gargantua and Pantagruel* Book I, chapters 52 ff.) with which Friar John of the Funnels is to be rewarded for his doughty services. Every detail in the design and management of the new abbey is the polar opposite of what is expected in abbeys. Thélème is not surrounded by walls and is constructed to afford the maximum of sunlight and air; real abbeys were walled and dark and dank. Real abbeys demand discipline; the motto of Thélème is "Do what thou wilt." The rules of real abbeys require obedience and poverty and chastity; in Thélème clocks (which mark the hours for offices) are forbidden, dress and food are as elegant and rich as possible, and monks and nuns inhabit the same building.—But what if a monk and nun should exchange coy glances or hold hands? The answer would be that if intelligent and well-nurtured people are naturally moved to do such things, it is not they but the rule which requires emendation. The revival of man the measure and of the distinction between nature and law or convention is plain and forceful. Man can only accommodate himself to nature, but conventions were created by men, and when they prove useless or injurious can be altered by men. Again the old dialogue is resumed where it was interrupted at the end of antiquity.

From their first appearance to this day the essays of Montaigne (1533–1592) have enjoyed a wide and continuous and intelligent readership, and they have been read not as curiosities or documents in intellectual history but as men read other mind-stretching books, for intellectual stimulation. This seems odd, for there is little in them that we do not already know or might indeed have said, if with much less skill and urbanity. But perhaps Montaigne's outlooks are part of the intellectual furniture of people who have not read Montaigne, as quotations from Matthew or *Hamlet* are familiar to people who have not read those books, because Montaigne *did* give them expression. Nor does the reader enjoy the excitement of watching an iconoclast at work; Montaigne does not thump the table or raise his voice to discredit the old and call attention to his own enlightened views, but speaks his mind with quiet assurance and so communicates the same assurance to his readers. His mild skepticism, his respect for the individual, his independence of authority all reflect the humanistic tradition. He makes no secret of his inspiration, but repeatedly acknowledges his obligations, as in these passages (from the translation by Florio, which Shakespeare used):

The Bookes that serve me are Plutarke, since he spoke French [the allusion is to Amyot's translation] and Seneca. . . . Seneca full-fraught with points and sallies, Plutarke stuft with matter.

From Plutarke or Seneca (as the Danaides) I draw my water, uncessantly filling, and as fast emptying.

What profit shall he not reap reading the lives of Plutarke? . . . To some kind of men it is a meere grammatical studie, but to others a perfect anatomie of Philosophie.

An essay in which the humanistic tradition is easily recognizable (and which shows analogies to *Utopia*) is "Of Cannibals," suggested by the report of a man who had sojourned in Brazil. Are the natives, whose usages are described, really barbarians?

Each man calls barbarism whatever is not his own practice. . . . Those people are wild, just as we call wild the fruits that Nature has produced by herself and in her normal course;

whereas really it is those that we have changed artificially and led astray from the common order, that we should rather call wild. . . . The very words that signify lying, treachery, dissimulation, avarice, envy, belittling, pardon, are unheard of among them.

They do kill and roast and feast on their captives, but Montaigne remarks:

I am not sorry that we notice the barbarous horror of such acts, but I am heartily sorry that, judging their faults rightly, we should be so blind to our own. I think there is more barbarity in eating a man alive than in eating him dead, in tearing by tortures and the rack a body still full of feeling, in roasting him bit by bit, having him bitten and mangled by dogs and swine (as we have not only read but seen within fresh memory, not among ancient enemies, but among neighbors and fellow-citizens, and what is worse, in the pretext of piety and religion) than in roasting and eating him after he is dead.

Elsewhere Montaigne says that a man must be very certain of his own convictions to destroy his fellow man for not agreeing with them. Three of the natives who attended a royal pomp in France were astonished at two things: first that so many stalwart men should submit to obey a puny king, and

secondly (they have a way in their language of speaking of men as halves of one another), that they had noticed that there were among us men full and gorged with all sorts of good things, and that their other halves were beggars at their doors, emaciated with hunger and poverty.

Man is the measure and conventions have no absolute. The irony of the closing sentence enforces the doctrine: "All this is not too bad. But wait! They don't wear trousers."

   Cervantes (1547–1616) destroyed the antiquated romances not by committing them to fire but by writing a far better one. But now the old is regarded not with contempt but with curiosity and compassion and even a touch of nostalgia; humanism could now embrace the nearer as well as the remoter past. What makes *Don Quixote* the first novel as well as the last medieval romance is that the Don and the lesser characters are not two-dimensional stalking images but convincing individuals, truly and lovingly drawn. The best of all illustrations of the dignity and independence of the individual is Don Quixote himself; instead of accepting the world about him he insists upon living in one he himself has fashioned. A few may sympathize with him and others gloat, but all envy him.

The three figures of the nineteenth century who have most affected modern outlooks upon man and the world—Darwin and Marx and Freud—are the clearest examples of the resumption of the intellectual dialogue where the ancients were interrupted. Darwin implies the differentiation of the realm of the supernatural and the realm of nature and the conception of nature as autonomous entity. Marx implies the distinction between *physis* and *nomos*: human institutions are the creation of men and their only sanction is what is expedient for man; when they are no longer expedient they should be changed. Freud implies the conception of man as a unit: the conflicts within man are not between the flesh and a detachable spirit but between the irrational chthonian and the rational Olympian elements which are both within man, or between his inalterable *physis* and the *nomos* to which he must conform.

As the work of these men and their successors shows, we are actually still in the humanist age. Changes in the political or social or intellectual climate induced by industrial or scientific revolution have affected interest in the ancient writings themselves. It has waned at times, and at times, as in the beginning of the nineteenth century and again in our day, it has received new attention and interpretation. But the work of the humanists has made it a central element in our culture, and so it must remain unless a revolution more total than any we have experienced extinguishes the tradition entirely.

CHAPTER 15.

THE GUARDIANS

To divide our educational curriculum into arts and sciences is not so meaningful as to divide it according to modes of approach and objectives. Science may not be so articulate as literature nor carry so broad a stream of humanistic tradition, but it is a highly important vehicle of intellectual activity and outlooks and so legitimately belongs with the humanities. Literature represents a wider range of interests and is accessible to a larger proportion of society, but when it is studied in a philological seminar it is scientific. The approach and objectives of the one kind of teaching are general education, in the language of current college catalogues, and of the other special education. The one kind is amateur, in the true sense (not dilettante or sciolist, as its opponents charge), and the other professional. The amateurs use their learning to enrich their lives, and only incidentally for gain. The lives of the professionals are also enriched, but they make a career of their learning. What is more important, they become the official guardians of the specialties they profess, not only in the sciences but in the arts also.

Among the Greeks, as we shall presently see, education was initially amateur and in only a few specialties which demanded expertise (and whose number gradually increased) was the approach professional. Among the peoples of the Near East which the Greeks encountered in the Hellenistic Age education was generally professional, and their example may have eventually accelerated the professionalization of Greek education also. Whereas Greek education, at least in the classical age, was designed to produce gentlemen amateurs, Eastern education was designed to perpetuate a guild of professional scribes. In Egypt where different types of writing, and in Mesopotamia where different languages, were used simultaneously, great technical proficiency was demanded of the scribe and his services were indispensable. He functioned not only in the bureaucracy but also as the keeper of specialized tradition. However widely learning might be shared among the population generally, the professional was its official guardian. He was set apart from other men.

For the traditions of culture the Greeks had no official guardians, nor, until the fourth century, formal institutions for propagating it. Training in handicrafts was a thing apart, as we have seen in Dame Culture's speech in Lucian. From the skill and taste revealed by surviving Greek artifacts we can surmise that craftsmen were given long and rigorous training, but we know few details. The word for teacher unqualified (*didaskalos*) means teacher of reading, and it was expected that his teaching would include moral instruction as well. The distinction between liberal and illiberal education is drawn by Aristotle in his *Politics* (1337b); it should be noted that "music" regularly includes literature:

There can be no doubt that children should be taught those useful things which are really necessary, but not all useful things; for occupations are divided into liberal and illiberal; and to young children should be imparted only such kinds of knowledge as will be useful to them without vulgarizing them. And any occupation, art, or science, which makes the body or soul or mind of the freeman less fit for the practice or exercise of virtue, is vulgar; wherefore we call those arts vulgar which tend to deform the body, and likewise all paid employments, for they absorb and degrade the mind. There are also some liberal arts quite proper for a freeman to acquire, but only in a certain degree, and if he attend to them too closely, in order to attain perfection in them, the same evil effects will follow. The object also which a man sets before him makes a great difference; if he does or learns anything for his own sake or for the sake of his friends, or with a view to excellence, the action will not appear illiberal; but if done for the sake of others, the very same action will be thought menial and servile. The received subjects of instruction, as I have already remarked, are partly of a liberal and partly of an illiberal character.

The customary branches of education are in number four; they are—(1) reading and writing, (2) gymnastic exercises, (3) music, to which is sometimes added (4) drawing. Of these, reading and writing and drawing are regarded as useful for the purposes of life in a variety of ways, and gymnastic exercises are thought to infuse courage. Concerning music a doubt may be raised—in our days most men cultivate it for the sake of pleasure, but originally it was included in education, because nature herself, as has often been said, requires that we should be able not only to work well but to use leisure well; for as I must repeat once again, the first principle of all action is leisure.

(Translated by BENJAMIN JOWETT)

From Homer's day onward the distinction of the *kalos k'agathos* ("gentleman") was his *paideia* ("culture"). Phoenix had been commissioned to teach young Achilles to be a proper doer of deeds and speaker of words; the first four books of the *Odyssey* are really concerned with the education of Telemachus to be a responsible and courteous gentleman. Like other aspects of the Homeric ethic the Homeric ideal of education for gentlemen prevailed in classical Greece also, and in the Athenian democracy a much larger proportion of the population could be gentlemen.

Education was in fact a principal concern of society, the whole of which was in a kind of conspiracy to see that the young were properly taught. In the *Protagoras* Plato makes Protagoras say:

Education and admonition commence in the first years of childhood, and last to the very end of life. Mother and nurse and father and tutor are vying with one another about the improvement of the child as soon as ever he is able to understand what is being said to him: he cannot say or do anything without their setting forth to him that this is just and that is unjust; this is honorable, that is dishonorable; this is holy, that is unholy; do this and abstain from that. And if he obeys well and good; if not he is straightened by threats and blows, like a piece of bent or warped wood. At a later stage they send him to teachers, and enjoin them to see to his manners even more than to his reading and music; and the teachers do as they are desired.

In Sparta a man was as responsible for admonishing and chastising a strange child as he was for his own.

What we should call elementary and secondary education was the responsibility of individuals; where the state took a hand was in the institution of the ephebate, of which young men became members at the age of eighteen. The purpose of the ephebate, which originated in Athens in the fifth century, was to initiate future citizens into their political, religious, and especially military duties, but it always included cultural subjects also. When the military became professional and Athens could no longer have an independent foreign policy the program became almost wholly cultural, with a heavy ingredient of athletics as a surrogate for military training. The authoritative account of the organization and function of the ephebate in its earlier form (though nothing is said of book-learning) is in Aristotle's treatise *On the Constitution of the Athenians* and worth quoting:

The present constitutional order is as follows: the right of citizenship belongs to those whose parents have been citizens. They are registered on the rolls of the demes at the age of eighteen. When they come up for enrollment, their fellow demesmen decide by vote under oath . . . whether the candidate is freeborn and of such parents as the law requires. . . . When the young men (*epheboi*) have passed this examination, their fathers assemble by tribes and, after having taken an oath, elect three of their fellow tribesmen over forty years of age whom they consider the best and the most suitable to supervise the young men. . . . These men then call the young men together and first make the circuit of the temples. Then they proceed to the Piraeus, and one part takes garrison at Munichia, the other at Acte.

The institution of the ephebate was adopted in all the Greek cities of the Hellenistic world, and the educational ideals promoted by *gymnasion* and ephebate informed the educational program in Rome and its successor states also.

If the Greeks had no scribes in the Eastern sense, the early epic poets did have a guild to foster and propagate their art, and the tragic poets regarded themselves and were regarded as teachers. The techniques of oral composition in the poetry of Homer must presuppose a professional group which preserved and cultivated those techniques over a long period of time. The Homerids (literally "sons of Homer") of whom we hear may have been such a professional guild. We now know that writing was known in Homeric times, though the art cannot have been common; perhaps the guild cared for the written libretti which were the basis for performances, which continued to be oral. Whether poets in other genres formed associations is doubtful; they plainly knew one another's work and sometimes there were family connections between them, especially in the case of writers of choral lyric, which preceded tragedy. Bacchylides was the nephew and protégé of Simonides, and Sophocles' son Sophron also composed tragedies. The function of the poet as teacher is evident in several forms but particularly in drama. In Aristophanes' *Frogs* Aeschylus is made to say: "Boys at school have a master to teach them; we poets are the teachers of men."

It may be that the conception of poet as authoritative teacher derived from the notion that poets are special spokesmen for the Muses. Hesiod and Pindar soberly declared that they were directly inspired, and down to the end of antiquity poets utter at least perfunctory invocations to the Muses. In several places, and especially in the *Ion,* Plato affirms his belief in inspiration, and in the *Phaedrus* he says: "Whoever knocks at the door of poetry without the Muses' incitement, persuaded that by art alone he will be a sufficient poet, fails of perfection, and the work of the sober is forthwith eclipsed by that of the frenzied." At least in the sense of receiving pay for their work the poets were professional; choral poets in particular—Simonides and Pindar and Bacchylides—received very large fees for their work.

How the work of the early philosophers was financed and organized we do not know. Thales was a successful businessman; the other Ionians may have been also, and may have taken paying pupils. In the West the Pythagorean brotherhood was self-sustaining, and Empedocles probably practiced medicine. For the pre-Socratics philosophy encompassed all knowledge and not merely what we call philosophy; Empedocles, for example, could write a poem "On Nature" and another "On Purifications." Socrates disclaims knowledge of science, but does not scorn it. Socrates himself notoriously accepted no fees for teaching, but Protagoras and the succession of Sophists demanded high fees. Best organized of all were the medical men at the Hippocratic school on the island of Cos. It was from this school that the communities of Greece obtained medical practitioners.

The first schools comparable to our own institutions of higher education were the Academy of Plato and the school of Isocrates, both founded early in the fourth century B.C., and the differences between them foreshadow the differences in our own institutions. Throughout his writings Plato advocates specialization of function and distrusts the nonprofessional, whether to train horses or play the flute or vote. His subject was philosophy in the narrower sense, but philosophy requires a trained capacity for reasoning, and therefore the Academy was much occupied with mathematics. Furthermore Plato believed that philosophy required long personal contact between master and disciple. He distrusted books, including his own. He excluded Homer and the tragic poets from his ideal Republic, and says, in his autobiographical Seventh Epistle, that anyone who presumed to learn his philosophy from books was mistaken. This meant that the Academy was exclusive as well as specialist.

Isocrates, who followed the Sophist tradition, taught oratory, with a view to success in public life, but oratory meant not only stylish composition but an understanding of social and political problems, of history, and indeed of all the concerns and outlooks of men. Just as speech should have proper style so should human activities reflected in speech have proper style also. The authoritative models for style, in political and social bearing as well as in expression, were to be found in literature; Isocrates trusted books and was an important agent in propagating them. His pupils probably far outnumbered Plato's; certainly they were more widely known and read. Almost all the orators and historians of the fourth century of whom we know were pupils of Isocrates. The new history was universal rather than local and sought to engage interest by dramatic and occasionally sensational treatment; its aim was edification as well as information. Plato was an incomparably more powerful intellect, and even as a writer he is immeasurably greater than Isocrates, but it may be a good thing that European education followed Isocrates' pattern rather than Plato's.

Aristotle sat at Plato's feet for twenty years before he developed his own philosophy and established the Lyceum (or Peripatetic School) to teach it. Whatever Aristotle may have rejected in Plato's teaching he accepted Plato's specialization and carried it very far indeed. Aristotle himself was encyclopedic—Dante aptly calls him the master of those that know—and he taught and wrote on many subjects, metaphysics and logic, ethics and politics, government, literature, physics, and others. One of his greatest contributions is that he differentiated separate disciplines, and laid down the methods of classification and analysis appropriate to each. A less spectacular though none the less significant contribution to science is that Aristotle made it respectable for a gentleman to do the ungentlemanly job of dissecting a fish for the sake of science.

Learning at so high a level must also have been exclusive and can have touched only a small proportion of the population directly; but now all systems of philosophy were obliged to have a physics and a logic, if only as a scaffolding for the ethics which was their chief concern. This was the case with Stoicism and Epicureanism, which did by design affect the lives of many men. For more effective teaching the Epicureans even reduced their doctrine to textbooks, probably following the example of Euclid, and even graded textbooks, the Smaller Epitome and the Greater.

The Peripatetic tradition of specialization was carried forward in Alexandria, which outstripped Athens as an intellectual center in the Hellenistic world. The Library and Museum at Alexandria comprised in effect a series of graduate institutes in which research of a high order was pursued in mathematics and astronomy and geography and anatomy and the like. Alexandrian study of literature became highly technical. Publication now falls into two categories, one addressed to fellow scholars and the other to popularization for nonspecialists. Aratus's good astronomical poem, the *Phainomena,* is a popularization of the work of professional astronomers like Eudoxus. The reason that the geocentric theory of the cosmos held the field until it was discredited by Copernicus and Galileo is that the popularizer Ptolemy (hence "the Ptolemaic system") chose the wrong astronomer to follow. Indeed Copernicus was put on the right track through his knowledge of better Alexandrian astronomers, like Hipparchus, who knew that the cosmos was heliocentric. But the spirit of specialization worked injury to the old ideal of the gentleman's education. In the old days any gentleman could accompany song on a musical instrument, now he must be a virtuoso; any gentleman could perform creditably on the playing field, now he must be a champion; any gentleman knew books, now he must be a philologer. If the professionalization of literary study sharpened the cleavage between gentleman and scribe, the scribe, as was noted in another connection, might attain special consideration both in this world and in the world to come.

Romans were keenly alive to class stratifications, and the gentry sensible of their responsibility to maintain the image appropriate to their class. When legal distinctions between patrician and plebeian were abolished there was even greater motivation to cut a proper figure—*far figura,* the Italians would say. The emphasis on gentleman's education was therefore very emphatic. No gentleman could engage in an occupation which required manual effort, and no gentleman could follow a profession which earned fees. Physicians and artists could be imported from Greece; the one profession in which the Romans themselves developed high efficiency was in the engineering of massive structures, including aqueducts and highways. It is a little distressing to find a man so devoted to Hellenism as Plutarch being so Romanized as to say that much as we admire the lyrics of Anacreon or the carvings of Phidias no sane man would think of making his son a musician or a sculptor. Sports, like drama, was a pastime for spectators. A gentleman would lose caste by acting or playing professionally. What annoyed the Romans about Nero was not that he fiddled while Rome burned (he probably did not), but that he fiddled at all, and acted, and took part in athletic contests, and said, "What an artist is here perishing," when he died, instead of being a spectator like a good Roman.

The most characteristic of Roman pursuits was the practice of law, and Roman lawyers took no direct fees. They were *patroni* or squires, and those who sought their help were *clientes* or dependents—who did of course express their "gratitude" in gifts and legacies. Philosophers were Greek, and Roman nabobs might keep a philosopher as a kind of domestic chaplain. Romans who undertook to write philosophic essays, like Cicero or Seneca, did so in the intervals of more important business; both men take pains to assert that they are amateurs, not professionals. Their philosophy is not speculative but mainly ethical, even in Cicero's treatises on government and on oratory. Science is an even worse case. Lucretius's *On the Nature of the Universe* shows not only knowledge but curiosity, but his materials are largely derived from his Epicurean sources and his object is not knowledge for its own sake but as a means to reinforce Epicurean teaching on the indifference of the gods to human affairs. The *Natural History* of the Elder Pliny is in the nature of an encyclopedia; its sources are Greek, and it adds nothing of the author's own. Massive as were Roman borrowings from Greek culture, science was not one of them.

But in the realm of literature, which is after all the main channel of the humanistic tradition, the Romans not only adopted Greek forms but also the Hellenistic canon of authentic classics and the Hellenistic reverence for that canon. Education was mainly literary. The elementary teacher was a *litterator* ("alphabet man"), and his business was to teach reading. The business of the *grammaticus* (we still say "grammar school") was to teach literature. Higher education was in the hands of a *rhetor*, but the themes the student wrote and discussed involved knowledge of history and geography and other matters as well as proper presentation of arguments. Those who could afford it went to Greece for sight-seeing and to hear lectures on "philosophy."

Preoccupation with literature and emulation of Greek studies soon produced a class of professional scholars in Rome also. The foremost scholar of Rome was Marcus Terentius Varro (116–27 B.C.), who was commissioned by Julius Caesar "to procure and classify the greatest possible libraries of Greek and Latin books and open them to the public." Varro's varied interests and accomplishments are mentioned in a fine address to him by Cicero (*Academics* 1.3.9):

'Tis you, Varro, who have revealed the life span of our fatherland, the descriptions of the ages, the laws of our sanctities and of our priesthoods, our discipline at home and in war, the situation of our territories and demesnes, the titles, species, functions, and causes of our usages sacred and profane; you have thrown most light upon our poets and upon Latin language and literature generally, and yourself have fashioned a composition varied and elegant in a wide choice of meters, and in many places have laid the basis for philosophy, if too slight for complete instruction, at least sufficient for instigation to further study.

As learning grew more specialist there appear the same tensions between professional and amateur which we are experiencing today. Here is Seneca (*Letter* 88) on scholarly hairsplitting:

It is no more to the point for me to investigate whether Homer or Hesiod was the older poet than to know why Hecuba, although younger than Helen, showed her years so lamentably. What would be the point in trying to determine the respective ages of Achilles and Patroclus? Do you raise the question, "Through what regions did Ulysses stray?" instead of trying to prevent ourselves from going astray at all times? We have no leisure to hear lectures on the question whether he was sea-tossed between Italy and Sicily or outside our known world.

But it is the distortions of scholarship that the amateur criticizes. "Leisure without study," he says elsewhere, "is death; it is a tomb for the living man." His elegant protreptic to study (in *Letter* 64) could hardly be bettered:

I worship the discoveries of wisdom and their discoverers; to enter, as it were, into the inheritance of many predecessors is a delight. It was for me they laid up this treasure; it was for me that they toiled. But we should play the part of a careful householder; we should increase what we have inherited. The inheritance shall pass from me to my descendants larger than before. Much still remains to do, and much will always remain, and he who shall be born a thousand ages hence will not be barred from his opportunity of adding something further.

Vespasian was the first to establish a regular salary for professors of Greek and Latin, and appointed Quintilian to a chair. Ausonius held a similar appointment in the fourth century; in that same century Donatus wrote his Latin grammar and commentaries on Terence and Vergil, and Servius his commentary on Vergil. The commentary of Macrobius (fifth century) on Scipio's Dream (at the end of Cicero's *Republic*) is Chaucer's point of departure for his *Parlement of Foules*. Macrobius's *Saturnalia* represents a group of scholars discussing various points of antiquarian lore. Macrobius is an important channel for transmitting ancient culture to the Middle Ages. More important for shaping European education is Martianus Capella's (sixth century) *Nine Books on the Marriage of Philology and Mercury and on the Seven Liberal Arts,* which was among the half dozen most widely circulated books in the Middle Ages. The standard Latin grammar was that of Priscian (early sixth century); Priscian is figured as representing grammar on the West Portal at Chartres. From the point of view of scholarship antiquity may be said to end in the year 529, when the monastery of Monte Cassino was opened and the School of Athens closed.

Of the course of learning during the Middle Ages and its revival during the Renaissance something has been said above, as also of the dramatic reinvigoration of the humanist tradition in the hands of the humanists. But not the least of their contributions was to the reform of education. We have seen how lively the process of learning was made in Erasmus's *Colloquies*. George Buchanan deplores the deadening effect of the dirty and mindless and heartless teachers of Paris in a poem called *Franciscanus*. Rabelais is devastatingly critical of the uncomprehending rote learning at the Sorbonne which was fatal to mind and spirit, and then outlines an enlightened program which included science and athletics and a full understanding of works of literature. Again there is tension between the professional guardians of learning and the amateurs. Montaigne, who had enjoyed a gentleman's education and is himself the ideal amateur, has an essay "On Pedantry" in which he expresses his impatience with men who call themselves "grammarians, not gentlemen."

It was the gentlemen who made the humanist tradition familiar to all literate men. What is notable about the famous battle of the books in England at the end of the eighteenth century is that virtually every man of letters involved himself in it, and that the proponents of Modern Learning could meet the defenders of Ancient Learning on their own ground. None could imagine that ancient learning should be abandoned. Latin was of course an essential, but the gentleman was expected to know Greek also, as we can see from a letter of Lord Chesterfield to his son:

Let Greek, without fail, share some part of every day: I do not mean the Greek poets, the catches of Anacreon, or the tender complaints of Theocritus, or even the porterlike language of Homer's heroes, of whom all smatterers in Greek know a little, quote often, and talk of always; but I mean Plato, Aristotle, Demosthenes, and Thucydides, whom none but adepts know. It is Greek that must distinguish you in the learned world, Latin alone will not.

As such a passage reveals, the object of study was often snobbish display, to demonstrate the interval by which the gentleman was set apart from the common herd. This attitude is properly satirized in some lines of Jonathan Swift:

> Get scraps of Horace from your Friends,
> And have them at your Fingers' Ends.
> Learn Aristotle's Rules by Rote,
> And at all Hazards boldly quote:
> Judicious Rymer oft review:

Wise Dennis and profound Bossu.
Read all the Prefaces of Dryden,
For these our Criticks much confide in,
(Tho' meerly writ at first for filling
To raise the Volume's Price a Shilling).
A forward Critick often dupes us
With sham Quotations Peri Hupsous;
And if we have not read Longinus,
Will magisterially outshine us.
Then lest with Greek he overrun ye,
Procure the book for Love or Money,
Translated from Boileau's translation,
And quote Quotation on Quotation.

Swift is himself a good example of the true vitality of the humanist tradition. But even if the motivation for the gentleman's education was sometimes dubious, the classics were studied and their precipitate became the possession of all literate people. How fully the classics permeated intellectual life can be seen from literature, much of which, on the Continent as in England, is imperfectly intelligible without familiarity with the tradition. When easy familiarity with it could be assumed, learned tags and allusions could serve as compendious symbols for communication. Much of the display of learning might be merely a superficial badge of class, but Pope's "the proper study of mankind is man" shows that more than words and forms came out of the humanistic tradition. The substance of the tradition might be invoked for various kinds of enlargement of spirit, especially in the romantic upsurge of interest in the classics at the beginning of the nineteenth century. Goethe could follow Greek form meticulously in his *Iphigenie auf Tauris* (which is far less Greek in spirit than Milton's *Samson Agonistes*), and something of Greek spirit in the second part of *Faust*. Byron could justify rebellion against one kind of suffocation in lines like

And thus they form a group that's quite antique,
Half-naked, loving, natural, and Greek.

In the middle of the nineteenth century, mainly in Germany, partly by the example of the burgeoning sciences and the methods of research appropriate to them, study of the ancients became so technical that it tended to become a closed preserve accessible only to professionals. Too often the professionals were so intent upon microscopic minutiae as to become oblivious to the larger significances of the humanistic tradition and its potentialities for liberation. But though classical study gradually lost its primacy in education, there were always devoted amateurs who realized the worth of the humanist tradition, and who eventually succeeded in restoring a reasonable balance. The simplest explanation for the survival of the classics is that ordinary readers have found them worth preserving.

CHAPTER 16
PROSPECTS

From the major crises which threatened its survival in the past the humanistic tradition emerged with increased strength and scope. In the Hellenistic Age it not only proved its capacity to transcend revolutionary change in social and political environment but took root and spread among peoples previously remote from it. In the humanist age it not only survived revolutionary scientific innovations but was strengthened by them. The revolution which we must now envisage will combine both kinds of change and be greater than their sum. At present the tradition is flourishing; can it again survive? Is it desirable that it should, and if so what means will promote its survival?

Both as an element in the educational process and as an agent in shaping outlooks and institutions the ancient humanistic tradition retains greater vitality than is commonly supposed. With the democratic expansion of educational opportunities and the restoration of liberal education, if not to the primacy usurped by science and technology, at least to a position of dignity, the number of people who have direct acquaintance with the ancient literary and artistic monuments has been greatly increased, not only absolutely but in proportion to the whole population. If the proportion of the educated who study the original language is much lower than it was a century ago, their number is by no means inconsiderable. Enough acquire sufficient expertness to carry on the scribal tradition. They as well as those who must approach the ancients through translations, are alive (as many of their predecessors were not) to the spiritual content of the tradition, not alone its vehicle.

The ancients are not merely an object of antiquarian curiosity, like artifacts of a forgotten past, looked at, as pyramids or Indian mounds are, across a gap of centuries. Reckoning by the calendar we are indeed remote from the Greeks, but reckoning by its expression in commonly accepted premises and outlooks and goals, the humanistic tradition which the Greeks originated and which defines Hellenism has never been stronger and more effective than it is today. Our discussion of the Greeks opened with a statement that "man is the measure of all things" is the salient characteristic of the Greek outlook, and the pages following sought to illustrate the implications of the doctrine in the high importance attached to individual man, and in religion, politics, literature, philosophy, and morality. Now the doctrine can no longer be called salient because it has become a generally accepted truism.

We make no question of the importance of individuals, though their numbers are a thousandfold greater than in the Aegean, and we cherish the ideal of *parrhesia* and *eleutheria*, free speech and liberty, as the Greeks did. And despite the enlargement we also honor the drive towards individual excellence and the distinction it brings. We give high recognition to talent, regardless of social position, and expect that creators' names be attached to their works. To safeguard the individual's rights and promote the full expression of his individuality the Greeks invented democracy; we have extended democracy by abolishing slavery and removing disabilities from women. It is an index to the universal acceptance of the democratic ideal that governments which are in fact authoritarian find it expedient to call themselves democracies. We are able to spread democracy and the participation in public life which it implies over enormously greater areas and populations because we have representative government (as the Greeks did not) and combine smaller units, which afford easier scope for assertion of individuality, into a large federation. The elected leader of such a federation has greater responsibilities than a Hellenistic monarch, but he pretends to no charismatic mystique. He is not master of his people but their servant.

"Of the gods I do not speak," Protagoras said, "because I cannot know." The corollary of the doctrine of man the measure is not atheism or even agnosticism, but a separation between the spheres of man and of the supernatural. The gods are not primarily concerned with surveillance over man, but lead their lives according to their own logic; and man too must behave as it becomes man to do, not by assimilation to an ideal outside of man. Because there were many gods with disparate spheres of interest it devolved upon man to determine which he would follow. There was nothing like an established church or a central religious authority. Here too men are nearer the Greeks than at any time since the end of antiquity. There is a pluralism of cults, church and state are separate, and the authority of institutional religion is diminished. Even among theologians there is much less certainty about the nature of the divine and its requirements of men. As among the Greeks, man may not be the master of his fate but he is captain of his soul.

Sophists of the fifth century believed in the essential equality of men of all races and degrees, and with Isocrates and the Stoics and Alexander and the Romans the ecumenical ideal of the unity of mankind sharing in a single organism and participating in common aspirations became an accepted part of the humanistic tradition. The humanists of Europe might dream of the ecumenical ideal but could do little to realize it. Now scientific advances justify our contemplating its realization. Increased abundance and speed of communication will eliminate distinctions between advanced and retarded areas, and exploration of outer space will make international tensions ridiculous. Mankind will perforce become closer knit, not through evangelical zeal but out of expediency. Like other strands in the humanistic strain the ecumenical ideal has not only survived but acquired increased vitality.

And finally, our prodigious scientific advances, though different in kind, are as original and seminal and as impressive in mass and pace as the towering intellectual achievements of the Greeks in their golden age. Whether the release of ingenuity and resourcefulness is a cause or an effect or merely a concomitant of the reinvigorated humanistic tradition, it is out of the humanist climate that the spirit of uninhibited inquiry derives, and perhaps our innovations are in fact the latest link in a chain whose beginnings the Greeks forged.

Can this be an Indian summer of humanism and a harbinger of a barren winter? From the point of view of increase of scientific knowledge and fuller control of environment and even of man's own nature, surely not. Though it fell into a lull after the Alexandrian spurt its progress has been steady all during the humanist era and will surely continue so as long as the humanist climate endures. But may not the very success of scientific progress crush the human elements in the humanistic tradition? Aside from the value of these elements for their own sake (of which something will be said presently), there may be practical reasons for preserving them, among them safeguarding science itself.

If the imminent revolution will not be so total as many well-informed people assure us it will be, still control of climate and fertility and manipulation of geography and biology are bound to affect society radically. But since we cannot divine the character and effects of the revolution, how can we prepare to cope with the problems it will present, or how shall we educate the young people upon whom the task will devolve to cope with them? There is a fragment in the poetry of Archilochus (who lived in the seventh century B.C.) which says: "The fox knows many things, the hedgehog one big thing." The one big thing the hedgehog knows—to roll himself into a ball and insulate himself from the world with a barrier of quills—can be taught; instinct or the hedgehog's mother is adequate to the task. But how teach the subtlety and versatility and improvisation which is foxiness? For men who must acquire foxiness the only prescription is the fullest possible knowledge of the experiences of the past: what challenges in society and politics, in science and art and all that concerns human life, confronted men in the past, and what kinds of responses did men devise? All of the experiences of the past are useful, but it may be that the Greek is most fruitful of all, because the Greeks were at once children and mature, logical and unsentimental and uninhibited, and because for them as for us man is the measure of all things.

The Greek pioneers and their successors whose basic theories have revolutionized thought may have been teachers or clerics or wards of rich patrons, but their theorizing was not calculated or predetermined or a necessary part of their jobs. Their theorizing was a form of play. Usually their discoveries resulted from a sudden realization of a connection between two things normally disparate—like a playful mind making puns or limericks. For the limericks to be arresting, the player needs not only ingenuity but a large fund of odd words and names. Some years ago the distinguished Dutch humanist Johan Huizinga wrote a playful and arresting book under the title *Homo Ludens,* implying that the proper designation for our species is not *Homo sapiens,* "man the intelligent," or *Homo faber,* "man the contriver," but "man the playful." Huizinga's subtitle is "A study of the play element in culture," and the implication of his work for us is that great conceptual innovations are produced not by grim men working on an assigned task but in a spirit of play. Syndicates of conscientious researchers thoroughly prepared to investigate and solve a defined problem are of course essential to scientific development, but we need foxes as well as hedgehogs, and will never know what we have lost, or what fine play we have deprived men of, if we abolish foxes.

If we measure civilization, as the ancients did, by degree of difference from the animal, science is as serviceable an index as poetry; a baboon can no more conceive of the nebular hypothesis than he can write *Paradise Lost*. Shared civilization, not physical likeness, is the common bond among men, and it would seem that the body of scientific knowledge would be adequate to this function. Scientists share a common reservoir upon which they base and to which they contribute their new findings; moreover they can share easily because their symbols of communication are more universal and more precise than the symbols of language. And yet a shared preoccupation with science can be an effective bond between remote people only if they share in other strands of the humanistic skein also. Scientific knowledge is not widely diffused and is unlikely ever to be; it engages too small a segment of the emotional gamut even in the competent, and it is too starkly intellectual to generate reciprocal warmth. When a new Nobel laureate in a scientific subject is announced, the nonspecialist press can say little that is generally intelligible of his technical achievement but fill their columns with "human interest" stories which are eagerly read. When a laureate in literature is announced there is often an intelligent appreciation of his work, frequently with significant quotations. The stream of humanistic tradition may be less pellucid than science but it is broader and warmer and more inclusive. It is, in short, the most effective avenue for mutual understanding among civilized men. What sense of unity mankind possesses is due to the shared stream of humanistic tradition, and since mankind will inevitably be drawn into closer proximity and interdependence it would seem reasonable to propagate rather than curtail a proven means to unity. No fabricated language has been able to take the place which Latin forfeited as a cultural medium for all Europe when Europe was fragmented, and no contrived device can serve to unite men as effectively as the humanistic tradition, which is deep-rooted and widely shared and has proven its cohesive power.

To maintain orderly existence in a world revolutionized by undreamt-of abundance and augmented population will require much regulation, with the consequence that individuality may be stunted. The best prophylactic against regimentation is the continuous awareness of the humanistic tradition which comes from books; that is why authoritarian regimes burn or censor books. In the regimented polities imagined by Plato in his *Republic* and by Huxley in his *Brave New World,* books like Homer and Shakespeare were banned, not because they are subversive, but because they stretch the mind, quicken sensibilities, open emotional pores. The uniform dun dress and identical houses in More's *Utopia* are tolerable only because there are books to safeguard individuality. Mass and abundance can be no threat to individuality if a man retains his human style, his capacity to think and feel subtly and profoundly, his knowledge of the tradition of which he is part. The unexamined life, Socrates said, is not worth living. How else examine it than in the light of the tradition to which man is heir?

That, in the last analysis, is the true reason for perpetuating the humanistic tradition; to justify it by its "practical" benefits is of a piece with justifying a game of chess on the ground that it teaches military tactics or keeps the player from more dangerous pastimes. The chess game is a legitimate end in itself, and so is awareness of the humanistic tradition also. The sole (and amply sufficient) goal of our quick march is the enhancement of human existence; if the result is impoverishment instead of enrichment then we are like tragic heroes striding unwitting to their doom, or rather like lemmings scampering madly to theirs. Prometheus will have been proved wrong in seeking to preserve the human race, and Zeus right in wishing to abolish it.

The Promethean way is the way of humanism. "The Athenians are addicted to innovation," Thucydides represents the Corinthians as saying. "They are adventurous beyond their power and daring beyond their judgment." Nor should latter-day humanists remain content with what they have out of fear of the unknown. Restless enterprise is indeed a part of the humanist tradition, which would be maimed if it were lulled to sleep. So firmly embedded is it in our outlooks that we assume it is a universal trait of civilized man, but other civilizations have preferred static tranquillity to progress made possible by technology. Here is a moral tale told by Chuang Tzu, who lived about 300 B.C.:

When Tzu Kung went South to the Ch'u State on his way to the Chin State, he passed through Han-yin. There he saw an old man engaged in making a ditch to connect his vegetable garden with a well. He had a pitcher in his hand, with which he was bringing up water and pouring it into the ditch—great labor with very little result.

"If you had a machine here," cried Tzu Kung, "in a day you could irrigate a hundred times your present area. The labor required is trifling as compared with the work done. Would you not like to have one?"

"What is it?" asked the gardener.

"It is a contrivance made of wood," replied Tzu Kung, "heavy behind and light in front. It draws up water as you do with hands, but in a constantly overflowing stream. It is called a wellsweep."

Thereupon the gardener flushed up and said: "I have heard from my teacher that those who have cunning implements are cunning in their dealings, and those who are cunning in their dealings have cunning in their hearts, and those who have cunning in their hearts cannot be pure and incorrupt, and those who are not pure and incorrupt are restless in spirit, and those who are restless in spirit are not fit vehicles for Tao. It is not that I do not know of these things. But I should be ashamed to use them."

The story is edifying, if only by reminding us that progress is a matter of choice, and the farmer is charming, but because he is a little absurd. It may be that Zeus denied man fire because he knew that with it the ultimate invention of a hydrogen bomb would be inevitable, and it may be that wiser things have been laboriously chiseled in stone (and with greater economy of words) than have been recorded on electronic tape; but new devices have steadily liberated rather than constricted, and there is no more reason to impose a moratorium on progress now than there was when the wheel was just invented. "Progress in the arts and in all other activities," wrote Isocrates (*Evagoras* 7), "comes not through those who cling to things as they are but through those who amend what is not as it should be and have the courage to change it."

Nor need we impose artificial scarcity for our souls' sake. Moralists have deplored the erosive effects of abundance upon character, and it was once the fashion to attribute the decline of Roman civilization to the spread of luxury. Today an ascetic may have sustenance superior in quality and variety and fetched from farther afield than might a Roman voluptuary. Another alleged reason for the decline of Rome is sheer size; Gibbon said that "the stupendous fabric yielded to the pressure of its own weight." If size and weight were the decisive factors the fabric might have disintegrated half a millennium earlier.

What makes men apprehensive of technology and abundance and mass is a fear that they may disrupt established values and established tradition. But civilization is an artificial structure. It stands upon the shoulders of the past, but it must also look to vitality in the future. An untended chick will peck as well as its mother; an untended infant, if it survives, will have to begin the whole process of civilization anew. The end result may be quite different from what we know, or if we accept the cyclical theory of history of the Greeks, our own history will be recapitulated. But a cycle is too long to wait; our capacities had better be used for advance than for recapitulation. Pagans like Symmachus and Rutilius who feared Christian dominance were not only concerned for the preservation of the accumulations of the past but feared that failure to attend to the tradition would obviate progress in the future. The legacy of the past is not a static thing. Merely to know what the ancients thought and said is not sufficient; the dialogue they started must be carried on. But not to know the past, as Cicero said, is to be forever a child, and a child is incapable of intelligent dialogue. A child has the potentiality of becoming a man; he realizes the potentiality not by mere physical growth but by acquiring the intelligence it behooves a man to have. He must learn how to subsist, but he must also learn what sets humanity apart from mere subsistence, and how men have asserted their humanity from the beginning. To be able to share in humanity he must be initiated into its tradition. His means to this end is the study of history, not alone political and economic history, but the history of literature and art, philosophy and science, the history of ideas. If he truly possesses his tradition he cannot do other than carry it forward, and no revolution in environment or social structure will be able to destroy his individuality.

Man's single most important enterprise is education. The enormously complicated machinery of our existence obviously requires specialists to operate it and will indubitably be more demanding in the future. But education in what are called the humanities is equally important, for unless the tradition will inform it, rising early to build the new house will be in vain. No one questions the need for education in science and technology, but neither should there be any question of the validity of humanistic education. Because its goal is the amateur rather than the professional, because its appeal is wider and all literate people, not teachers alone, contribute to its propagation, humanistic education is in itself more viable and may stand in less need of patronage to assure its survival. But it does need recognition and esteem and it does need ever-widening diffusion among those who are not its direct heirs or who have forsaken their legacy. The need is especially urgent when competing interests are so conspicuously successful as to put the validity of the humanistic tradition into question. But as tradition has survived past crises so it will survive the emergent crisis also. Tradition does have a future.

INDEX

Athenians, appraisal of, by Corinthians, 48–49, 187
Augustine, Saint, 114, 144
Augustus, 117, 120
Ausonius, 144, 176

Bacchylides, 169, 170
Barbarians, 105, 107; Montaigne on, 162–63
Basil the Great, 140
Battle of the books in England, 177
Bede, Venerable, 145
Belles lettres, 77, 83, 129, 156
Bembo, Cardinal Pietro, 146–47
Biblical archaeology, 110
Biblical canon, books in, 111
Biographies, individualities recorded in, 152
Biological engineering, potentialities of, 2
Birds (Aristophanes), 54
Boccaccio, Giovanni, 153, 156
Boiardo, Matteo Maria, 153
Books: as prophylactic against regimentation, 186; of non-Greeks, Hellenism influence on, 103; as repository of Greek style, 71–72, 78
Bourgeois types in literature of Hellenistic revolution, 96
Brave New World (Huxley), 186
Bribery, Greek attitude toward, 20
Buchanan, George, 153, 176
Byron, George Noel Gordon, 178
Byzantine culture, dissemination of, 142

Caesar, Julius, 117, 174
Callimachas, 96
Callinus of Ephesus, 19, 42–43
Camillus, 121
Camoëns, Luis de, 153
Canons of ancient Greek books, 71
Capella, Martianus, 176
Carolingian revival of learning, 142, 145
Catholic Church, and Roman influence on Europe, 143–44
Cavalry, in Athenian democracy, 46
Cellini, Benvenuto, 152
Cervantes, 163–64

Chapman, George, 87
Charlemagne, 142
Chaucer, Geoffrey, 176
Chinese ideograph, xvi
Choral lyrics of Greece, 82, 169
Christiads (Vida), 152, 153
Christianity: hostility of, to Hellenism, 104, 107; and humanistic tradition, 113–14; and pagan classics, 140–41; and Roman humanism, 124–26, 144–45
Christus Patiens (Gregory of Nazianus), 78
Chuang Tzu, 187
Cicero, 59, 66, 119, 133, 174, 175, 189
Ciceronianism, 146–47
Cities of Greek pattern, in Hellenistic Age, 99
Citizen, in Athenian democracy, 95
City of God, The (Augustine), 144
City-states of Greeks, 69, 94–95
Civilization: measure of, 70–71, 185; Persian, 109; role of Greek style in, 132; Roman, decline of, 188; sharing of, 185; see also European civilization; Greek civilization
Class distinctions, 27, 173
Classics: Greek, 81–82, 87–88, 129; and library at Alexandria, 79; permeation of intellectual life by, 178–79
Claudius Claudianus, 144
Clement of Alexandria, 140
Clouds (Aristophanes), 28–29
Code of style, see Style
Coined money, introduction of, 43
Cola di Rienzi, 150
Colloquies (Erasmus), 158, 176
Comedy, realism of, 82; traditional form in, 83
Competition, Hesiod on, 33
Constantine the Great, 143
Contradiction, Law of, 90, 155
Copernicus, Nicholas, 172
Covenant of Hebrews, 111–12
Crates, 55–56
Cult of the hero, see Heroes
Cultural interchange between East and West, 115
Curtius, Ernst, 136
Cynics, 55, 101, 115

Dante Alighieri, 123, 148, 171
Daphnis and Chloe (Longus), 54
Darius, 62
Dark Ages, 144–45
Darwin, Charles, 67, 164
Deification of kings, 97–98
Delian League, 45–46
Delphi, 45, 131
Demetrius of Phalerum, 92
Democracy: of today, 181–82; *see also* Athenian democracy
Demosthenes, 50
Descartes, René, 154, 155
Dialogues, as literary form, 83–84, 164
Diogenes, 55
Diotima, 23
Disabilities imposed by sex and status, 30
Discourses on the First Ten Books of Livy (Machiavelli), 157
Divine Comedy (Dante), 148
Don Quixote (Cervantes), 163–64
Donatus, 176
Dostoevsky, F. M., xvi
Drama: of humanist age, 79, 152–153; traditional form in, 92, 93
Druidism, 135
Dualism of body and soul, 32, 107

East: aesthetic values in, 113; and anonymity, 151; and Greece, early affinities between, 107; Hellenization of, 98–100, 132–33; influence upon West, 114; major increments from, 113; professional education in, 165–66
East Greek culture, transmission of, 139–40
Ecclesiastes, 104, 115
Ecclesiasticus, 103
Eclogues (Vergil), 134
Ecumenical ideal of unity of mankind, 26–27, 61–67, 182, 185–86
Education: amateur and professional, 165–66; of a gentleman, 172–73, 178; liberal and illiberal, Aristotle on, 166–67; Plato on, 167–68; reform of, by humanists, 176–77; today's need for, in the humanities, 189–90; *see also* Greek education

Egalitarianism, 40–41
Egbert, Archbishop of York, 145
Electra (Euripides), 30, 77
Electra (Sophocles), 77
Elegiac couplet form, 82
Empedocles, 53, 170
English language, Latin elements in, 139
Ennius, Quintus, 97
Enupnion (Lucian), 91, 130
Ephebate, institution of, 168–69
Epic: form fixed by Homer, 81, 82; in the humanist age, 153–54; major epic of Alexandrian age, 85–86; and propagating heroic outlook, 79–80
Epicharmus, 83–84
Epicureans, 8, 38, 57–58, 66, 96, 101, 172
Epistles, as literary form, 83, 92
Erasmus, 67, 92, 143–44, 147, 157–159, 176
Eratosthenes, 64–65
Essenes, 111
Ethics (Aristotle), 52
Euclid, 172
Eudoxus of Cnidus, 172
Euhemerus, 97, 160
Eumenides (Aeschylus), 14, 36
Euripides, 11, 14, 16, 27, 28, 29–30, 31, 76, 83, 96, 104, 151
European civilization, and the Greeks, 6; and the Romans, 134
European culture, and the Greeks, 5, 106
European drama: influence of Seneca on, 78–79, 92; and traditional form, 92–93
European epic: and Greek heroic image, 80; influence of Homer and Vergil on, 81–82
European Literature of the Latin Middle Ages (Curtius), 136
European political climate, influence of Vergilian premises on, 113
European tradition of elegant epistolography, 92
Eusebius of Caesarea, 88, 143
Euthyphro (Plato), 53–54
Evagoras (Isocrates), 23
Exagoge (Ezekielos), 78
Ezekielos, 78

Fame, obsession of Greeks with, 23–24
Fate, power of, over the gods, 11
Firearms, invention of, 5, 148
Folk literature, of Athens, 84
Franciscanus (Buchanan), 176
Freud, Sigmund, 67, 164
Frogs (Aristophanes), 169
Fronto, Marcus Cornelius, 89
Funeral Oration of Pericles, 47
Future world, conception of, 36–37

Galileo, 172
Gargantua and Pantagruel (Abbey of Thélème), 161
Gentleman: education of, 172–73, 178; Roman standards for, 173
Geocentric theory of universe, 4, 172
Georgics (Vergil), 134
Gibbon, Edward, 143, 188
Gilgamesh epic, 107, 109, 113
Giraldus Cambrensis, 146
Glory, as motivation of Greeks, 23, 41
"Godly Feast, The" (Erasmus), 159
Gods of the Greeks: behavior of, 11–14; intervention on behalf of mortals, 15; lives of, 10; occupation of separate sphere from man, 32, 155, 182
Goethe, Johann Wolfgang von, 178
Gorgias of Leontini, 83
Gorgias (Plato), 104
"Grand Inquisitor, The" (Dostoevsky), xvi
Greek civilization, style as measure of, 70–71
"Greek," definition of term, 69–70
Greek education: designed to produce gentlemen amateurs, 165–166; Homer as mainstay of, 71–74; Isocrates' educational program, 129; Lucian on *paideia*, 130; Plato on, 128; in style, 71; tragedy as essential of, 76–77
Greek style: books as repository of, 71–74; code of, 40, 68–80; education of Greeks in, 71; Homer as mainstay of, 72; Homeric legacy of, 81
Greek values, perpetuation of, in non-Greek lands, 40

Gregory of Nazianzus, 78
Gregory of Nyssa, 140
Gregory, Pope, the Great, 145
Gregory of Tours, 145
Grillparzer, Franz, 87
Guilt, as communal and hereditary, 33, 36
Gymnasion, 99, 100, 102, 129, 169

Hammurabi, code of, 109
Handicrafts, Greek training in, 166
Hard work, Hesiod on, 33
Hebrew Scriptures, translation of, into Greek, 88–89, 132–33
Hebrews, and Greek culture, 102
Hecataeus, 62
Heliocentric theory of universe, 4, 148
Hellenism: and the Bible, 110; cult of, 127
Hellenistic Age: revolution of, 94–115; and survival of humanistic tradition, 7, 40, 94, 129–30, 148, 180; and theory of equality of all men, 124; utopias written in, 160
Heraclitus, 63
Hermogenes of Tarsus, 89–90, 91
Hero and Leander (Musaeus), 86–87
Herodotus, 44, 62, 103, 107, 109, 132, 160
Heroes: Euripides' discredit of heroic legend, 30, 76–77; Greek attitude toward, 15–16, 18–19, 75–77; of the Greek tragedies, 16–19, 75–77; of Homer, 72–75; persistence of ideal of heroic age, 86
Herondas, 85, 96
Hesiod, 11, 23, 24, 32–33, 38, 39, 42, 43, 74, 76, 169
Hipparchus, 172
Hippocrates, 26
Hippocratic school of medicine, 170
Hipponax, 82, 85
Historia ecclesiastica gentis Anglorum (Bede), 145
History of the Franks (Gregory), 145
History: linear progression of, 115; recurrent cycles of, 114, 188; study of, 189
Homer, 8, 11, 14, 26, 32–33, 41–42, 61, 71–75, 82, 169, 196
Homerids, 169

Law, Roman practice of, 173–74
Laws (Cicero), 119
Letter writing, as literary form, 83, 92
Libanius, 92
Life of Apollonius of Tyana (Philostratus), 88
Light-armed troops, in Athenian democracy, 46
Literary artistry of the East, 113
Literary criticism of humanist age, 152
Literary scholarship, in Common Era, 90–91
Literary style: as Homeric legacy, 81; in humanist age, 150–51; innovations in, 85, 86
Literature: Alexandrian study of, 172; Byzantine, 89–90, 91–92; in Greek education, 127–28, 129; of Greeks, and sack of Constantinople, 142–43; of Hellenistic revolution, 96; of humanist age, 152; as main channel of humanistic tradition, 174; Roman, 122–23, 133–34, 174; study of history of, 189
Livius Andronicus, 133–34
Livy, 114, 120, 122
Logos, as common gauge of humanity, 63, 69
Longus, 54
Lucian of Samosata, 87, 91, 130, 133, 156, 160, 166
Lucretius, 38–39, 134, 174
Lusiads (Camoëns), 153
Luther, Martin, 143–44
Lyceum, of Aristotle, 128, 170–71

Maccabees, Books of, 102, 103, 104, 151
Machiavelli, Niccolò, 67, 156–57
Macrobius, 145, 176
Man: as captain of his soul, 32, 182; development of, scientific and theologic views on, 61; enhanced importance of, 149–50
Man the measure, doctrine of, 8–24, 181, 182, 184
Map, Walter, 146
Marcus Aurelius, 56, 67, 89, 134
Marlowe, Christopher, 87
Marx, Karl, 67, 164

Materialism of Epicureans, 57, 66
Medea (Euripides), 30, 77, 151, 153
Meekness, lack of, in the Greeks, 22
Menander, 96
Metaphysics (Aristotle), 52
Middle Academy, of Hellenistic Age, 95
Middle Ages, culture of, 136–37, 176
Migrations of Hellenistic revolution, 94, 98
Milton, John, 154, 178
Mime writers, 85
Mimes (Herondas), 85
Molière, Jean Baptiste Poquelin, 153
Montaigne, Michel Eyquem de, 67, 132, 153, 161–63, 177
Monte Cassino, monastery of, 176
More, Thomas, 4, 67, 159–61, 186
Musaeus, 86–87
Mysticism, of Neoplatonists, 59

Names, importance attached to, 151–152, 181
National consciousness, in humanist age, 24
Nationalism, in Greece and Rome, 124
Natural History (Pliny), 174
Nature/convention dichotomy, 25–39
Navy, in Athenian democracy, 46–47
Near East, and man's cultural history, 110
Near Eastern thought, affinities of Hesiod to, 39
Neoplatonists, 59, 95, 120
New Academy, of Hellenistic Age, 59
New Comedy, realism of, 77, 82, 83, 96
Nine Books on the Marriage of Philology and Mercury and on the Seven Liberal Arts (Capella), 176
Non-Greek tradition, and heroic Greek ideal, 78
North's version of Plutarch, 132

Odyssey (Homer), 11, 42, 71–72, 134, 167
Oedipus at Colonus (Sophocles), 31
Oedipus the King (Sophocles), 18, 31
"Of Cannibals" (Montaigne), 162

Prince (Machiavelli), 157
Printing, invention of, 5, 148
Priscian, 176
Professional scholars in Rome, 174–175
Professionals and amateurs, tension between, 175, 177
Progress, and the humanist tradition, 187–88
Prometheus, myth of, 3, 39, 148, 187
Prose, of Isocrates, 77–78, 83
Protagoras (Plato), 128, 167
Protagoras, the Sophist, 8, 9, 63, 170, 182
Prudentius, 125–26, 144
Pseudepigrapha, 103
Ptolemaic system, 172
Ptolemies, and cultivation of Greek literature, 84
Pulci, Luigi, 153
Purifications (Empedocles), 53, 170
Pythagoras, 36, 53
Pythagorean brotherhood, 170
Pythagoreanism, 59, 90

Quintilian, 176
Quintus of Smyrna, 36
Qumran sectarians, 111

Rabelais, François, 67, 161, 176–77
Race: distinctions of, 24–25, 61; intelligence vs. race as criterion of superiority, 25–26, 63, 67, 70
Racine, Jean, 153
Regimentation, books as prophylactic against, 186
Religion: and Hellenization of East, 101–2; polytheism of Greeks, 10–11, 14; Roman attitudes toward, 118–20; today's status of, 182; see also Christianity; Gods of the Greeks
Religion: and Hellenization of East, ian and centralized, 113
Republic (Cicero), 176
Republic (Plato), 27, 37, 38, 160, 186
Republic (Zeno), 56, 66
Revolution: dimensions of, 2; in Hellenistic Age, 40, 94–115, 148, 180; in humanistic age, 148, 180; and survival of humanistic tradition, 1–3, 40, 56, 148, 180; in

world today, 2–3, 148, 180, 183–84
Rienzi, Cola di, 150
Roman influence in present public life, 123
Romance: in the humanistic age, 162–63; traditional form in, 92, 93
Romance languages, 136, 139
Rome: Aeneid as institutional poem of, 80, 112–13, 120; ancient history of, 120; charter of, 68, 112; and Christianity, symbiosis of, 144–45; class stratifications in, 173; codes of law, 124; deification of emperors, 97–98; and the ecumenical ideal, 66–67, 182; and Greek classics, 87–88; and Greek cultural legacy, 133; political and religious organization of empire, 114; provincial administration of, 134–35; and Roman style, 116–26; stability of, 116–17, 122; and survival of humanistic tradition, 127–37; universality of, 124
Rutilius Namatianus, 125, 189

Samson Agonistes (Milton), 178
Sappho, 36
Sarapis, cult of, 101
Saturnalia (Macrobius), 145, 176
Scaliger, Julius Caesar, 152
Schiller, J. C. F. von, 87
Scholar-poets of Alexandria, 84
School of Isocrates, 129, 170, 171
Science: status of, in Roman culture, 174; study of history of, 189; today's advances in, 183, 185
Scipio Aemilianus, 114–15
Scribes, professional, of the East, 166
Sculpture, 133
Second Sophistic movement, 87, 146
Seneca, 78–79, 83, 92, 133, 134, 174, 175
Sentimentality, as suspect to Greeks, 39, 86
Septuagint, 88, 133
Servius, 176
Seven against Thebes (Aeschylus), 75
Seven Books Against the Pagans (Orosius), 144
Shakespeare, William, 132, 153, 186
Sidonius Apollinaris, 145

Signatures as index of humanism, 23–24, 151
Simonides of Ceos, 169, 170
Slavery, and nature/convention dichotomy, 31
Socrates, 21, 23, 27, 31, 53, 54, 64, 186
Solon, 23, 34–36, 43, 75, 82
Sophists, 9, 25, 26, 27, 28, 31, 38, 170, 171, 182
Sophocles, 16, 21, 30, 31, 49–50, 63, 75, 76, 77, 96, 169
Sophron, 83–84, 169
Specialization, advocacy of: in Alexandria, 172; by Aristotle, 171; by Plato, 170
Spheres of man and the supernatural, separation of, 32, 155, 182
Spinoza, Baruch, 154, 155
Spiritual values, and humanistic tradition, 139
Statuary, 133
Stoicism, 19, 39, 55–57, 59, 66, 96, 101, 114, 115, 124, 155–56, 172, 182
Strabo, 64
Style: institutional authority for, 91; as measure of civilization, 71; new attention to, in Renaissance, 150; philosophy affected by excessive concern for, 90; precedence of, over content, 89; Roman, 116–126; as sole criterion of literary merit, 87; traditions of, 4; *see also* Greek style; Rome, Roman style
Suppliants (Aeschylus), 12–13
Swift, Jonathan, 177–78
Symmachus, 125, 144, 188–89
Symposium (Plato), 23, 132
Synesius of Cyrene, 140–41

Tarn, W. W., 55
Tasso, Torquato, 153
Terence, 134, 137, 176
Teseide (Boccaccio), 153
Thales, 170
Thaumaturgy, 95, 120

Thélème, Abbey of, 161
Themistocles, 20, 45
Theocritus, 85, 96
Theognis of Megara, 74–75, 82
Thrasymachus, 27
Thucydides, 27–28, 47, 53, 63, 124, 156, 187
Timaeus (Plato), 114
Trachinian Women (Sophocles), 77
Tragedy, stylized character of form, 82, 83
Treason, Greek attitude toward, 20–21
Trial by jury, 14, 36
Trojan Women (Euripides), 28, 104
True History (Lucian), 160
Tyrants, rise of, 43–44
Tyrtaeus of Sparta, 19, 42–43

Ugaritic writings, 109, 113
Unity of mankind, 26–27, 61–67, 182, 185–86
Utopia (More), 159–60, 162, 186
Utopia, and tradition of humanity, 4, 160

Varro, Marcus Terentius, 174–75
Vasari, Giorgio, 152
Vergil, 74, 80, 81, 123, 134, 152, 176
Vespasian, 176
Vida, Jerome, 152, 153

Waning of the Middle Ages, The (Huizinga), 149
West: Byzantium influence on, 142–143; Romanizing of, 135–36
Wisdom of Sirach, 103
Wisdom of Solomon, 103
Works and Days (Hesiod), 32, 37, 39, 42

Xenophanes, 11
Xenophon, 21, 107

Zeno of Citium, 55–56, 66

About the Author

Moses Hadas was one of the world's great classical scholars—the author of such distinguished works as *A History of Greek Literature* (1950), *A History of Latin Literature* (1952), *Hellenistic Culture* (1959) and *Humanism* (1960). He was born in Atlanta, Georgia, in 1900 and received his B.A. degree from Emory University and his M.A. and Ph.D. degrees from Columbia University. He held the chair of Jay Professor of Greek at Columbia University. Professor Hadas died in August, 1966.

About the Editor

Ruth Nanda Anshen, philosopher and editor, plans and edits Perspectives in Humanism, World Perspectives, Religious Perspectives, Credo Perspectives, and The Science of Culture Series. She writes and lectures on the unity of knowledge in relation to the unity of man.